FRANCIS FRITH'S

# COWES TOWN AND CITY MEMORIES

THE FRANCIS FRITH COLLECTION

www.francisfrith.com

FRANCIS FRITH'S
**TOWN** *&* **CITY**
MEMORIES

# COWES

**VALERIE McGEE** is a Southern Tourist Board Registered Tour Guide.
She has an extensive interest in local history; she has also co-written and
published a guide book relating the life and experiences of Alfred the Great.
Since her move to Lymington, she has developed a strong interest in the Isle
of Wight and the New Forest. The maritime history of the area has become
part of that interest, leading her inevitably to a fascination with Cowes.

THE FLOATING BRIDGE 1897 40368A

FRANCIS FRITH'S
TOWN & CITY
MEMORIES

# COWES

VALERIE McGEE

First published as Cowes, A Photographic History of your Town
in 2001 by Black Horse Books, an imprint of The Francis Frith Collection
Revised paperback edition published in the United Kingdom in 2005 by
The Francis Frith Collection as Cowes, Town and City Memories
ISBN 978-1-84589-513-6

British Library Cataloguing in Publication Data

Cowes
Town and City Memories
Valerie McGee

The Francis Frith Collection®
Frith's Barn, Teffont,
Salisbury, Wiltshire SP3 5QP
Tel: +44 (0) 1722 716 376
Email: info@francisfrith.co.uk
www.francisfrith.com

Aerial photographs reproduced under licence from Simmons Aerofilms Limited
Historical Ordnance Survey maps reproduced under licence from Homecheck.co.uk

Printed and bound in England

Front Cover: **COWES, THE OLD PIER 1950** C173011t
The colour-tinting in this image is for illustrative purposes only,
and is not intended to be historically accurate

# FRANCIS FRITH'S
# TOWN & CITY
### MEMORIES

## CONTENTS

Francis Frith, Victorian founder of the world-famous photographic archive, was a devout Quaker and a highly successful Victorian businessman. By 1860 he was already a multi-millionaire, having established and sold a wholesale grocery business in Liverpool. He had also made a series of pioneering photographic journeys to the Nile region. The images he returned with were the talk of London. An eminent modern historian has likened their impact on the population of the time to that on our own generation of the first photographs taken on the surface of the moon.

Frith had a passion for landscape, and was as equally inspired by the countryside of Britain as he was by the desert regions of the Nile. He resolved to set out on a new career and to use his skills with a camera. He established a business in Reigate as a specialist publisher of topographical photographs.

Frith lived in an era of immense and sometimes violent change. For the poor in the early part of Victoria's reign work was a drudge and the hours long, and ordinary people had precious little free time. Most had not travelled far beyond the boundaries of their own town or village. Mass tourism was in its infancy during the 1860s, but during the next decade the railway network and the establishment of Bank Holidays and half-Saturdays gradually made it possible for the working man and his family to enjoy holidays and to see a little more of the world. With characteristic business acumen, Francis Frith foresaw that these new tourists would enjoy having souvenirs to commemorate their days out. He began selling photo-souvenirs of seaside resorts and beauty spots, which the Victorian public pasted into treasured family albums.

Frith's aim was to photograph every town and village in Britain. For the next thirty years he travelled the country by train and by pony and trap, producing fine photographs of seaside resorts and beauty spots that were keenly bought by millions of Victorians.

## THE RISE OF FRITH & CO

Each photograph was taken with tourism in mind, the small team of Frith photographers concentrating on busy shopping streets, beaches, seafronts, picturesque lanes and villages. They also photographed buildings: the Victorian and Edwardian eras were times of huge building activity, and town halls, libraries, post offices, schools and technical colleges were springing up all over the country. They were invariably celebrated by a proud Victorian public, and photo souvenirs – visual records – published by F Frith & Co were sold in their hundreds of thousands. In addition, many new commercial buildings such as hotels, inns and pubs were photographed, often because their owners specifically commissioned Frith postcards or prints of them for re-sale or for publicity purposes.

In order to gain some understanding of the scale of Frith's business one only has to look at the catalogue issued by Frith & Co in 1886: it runs to some 670 pages. By 1890 Frith had created the greatest specialist photographic publishing company in the world, with over 2,000 stockists! The picture on the right shows the Frith & Co display board on the wall of the stockist at Ingleton in the Yorkshire Dales (left of window). Beautifully constructed with a mahogany frame and gilt inserts, it displayed a dozen scenes.

### POSTCARD BONANZA

The ever-popular holiday postcard we know today took many years to appear, and F Frith & Co was in the vanguard of its development. Postcards became a hugely popular means of communication and sold in their millions. Frith's company took full advantage of this boom and soon became the major publisher of photographic view postcards.

Francis Frith died in 1898 at his villa in Cannes, his great project still growing. His sons Eustace and Cyril continued their father's monumental task, expanding the number of views offered to the public and recording more and more places in Britain, as the coasts and countryside were opened up to mass travel. The archive Frith created continued in business for another seventy years. By 1970 it contained over a third of a million pictures of 7,000 cities, towns and villages. The massive photographic record Frith has left to us stands as a living monument to a special and very remarkable man.

This book shows your town as it was photographed by this world-famous archive at various periods in its development over the past 150 years. Every photograph was taken for a specific commercial purpose, which explains why the selection may not show every aspect of the town landscape. However, the photographs, compiled from one of the world's most celebrated archives, provide an important and absorbing record of your town.

COWES FROM THE AIR 1923 AF39662

The Harbour c1871 5746

Below left to right: 60499, 32838, 66313 & 40368a

A traveller crossing the waters of the Solent from mainland Britain may sometimes feel irresistibly drawn to the Island rising out of the sea. It was called Ynys yr wyth in ancient times, and is known today as the Isle of Wight. During its long history, the little island was renamed Vectis when it was invaded by the Romans under Vespasian. It was savagely attacked by the rampaging tribes of Jutes, Saxons and Danes for spoils of war and land. However, after the arrival of the Normans in 1066, the Island has never again been dominated by foreign armies, although throughout the centuries it has been threatened by forces from the Continent many times.

The origin of the name Cowes is unclear. It has been suggested that the name originally came from a sandbank called a 'cowe' which was outside the harbour. Another possibility is that the name came from the two castles, sometimes referred to as 'cows,' built by Henry VIII on either side of the estuary as part of his coastal defences.

Of the fort at East Cowes there is no trace, but the Royal Yacht Squadron, the most famous yacht club in the world, has made its home in the castle at Cowes. There were earlier small settlements here called East and West Shamblord, but it was the shield of Henry's forts that prevented French raids, allowing the towns either side of the River Medina to develop. The River Medina is navigable for six miles inland as far as Newport, the county town. In 1816 the town on the west bank was officially named West Cowes; the name was changed to Cowes in 1895.

The town's fame as a yachting haven was rapidly established after the formation of the Royal Yacht Squadron in 1833. When, in 1845, Queen Victoria bought Osborne House in East Cowes as a family home she could retreat to, Cowes became extremely fashionable as a holiday resort as well.

# INTRODUCTION

THE REGATTA 1903 50797C

The deep and sheltered waters known as Cowes Roads, leading to the small harbour at the mouth of the River Medina, were instrumental in the development of Cowes as a yachting mecca and of East Cowes for shipbuilding. Wooden ships were built at Cowes as long ago as the 16th century. Indeed, after the Spanish Armada ceased to be a threat, ships would drop anchor in the natural harbour to stock up with supplies before they made their often treacherous voyages across uncharted seas.

# INTRODUCTION

THE PARADE C1871 5749

# THE PARADE

There are very few small seaside towns in the world, that can boast of a more illustrious list of visitors than Cowes. The Parade, which is on the seafront overlooking the Solent, is at the heart of this yachting mecca, and is the home of the world-renowned Royal Yacht Squadron. Indeed, the ornate stone balustrade by the water's edge seems to have been purpose-built for the arms of those people who gaze out to the Solent to look at boats and ships of every kind. Moreover, it is a timeless place; it is fascinating to wander where history, tragedy and enjoyment have mingled.

The Parade was opened as the Victoria Parade on 22 June 1897 to commemorate the Diamond Jubilee of Queen Victoria. As it stands today, the Parade is very similar in character to when it was refurbished, over 100 years ago. However, some buildings have changed, cars and coaches have taken the place of donkeys and carts, and a pier has been built and demolished.

The hotel industry was developed to cater for the beginning of the tourist trade, although the boom in yachting overwhelmed any real attempt to open the town as a simple holiday resort. Sea-bathing was encouraged, but currents are strong and the shoreline is steep.

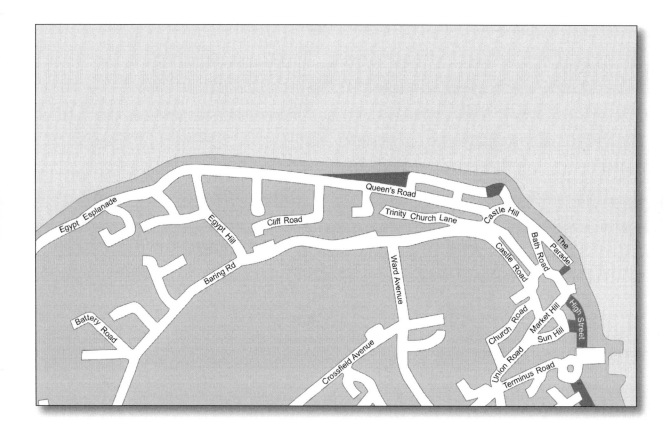

ABOVE: FROM THE SOLENT 1897  40367

At the east end of the Parade, by the last slipway, is the Island Sailing Club (left), which was founded in 1889, and is amongst the largest in the world. Upholding the ideas of emancipation, it was one of the first to admit women. The Duke of Edinburgh is an eminent member of this club. Next to the club, on the corner of the Parade and Watch House Lane, is the Watch House of HM Customs. This has played a very important part in the history of Cowes, and continues to do so.

LEFT: DETAIL FROM 40367

The first house at the east end of the Parade is Townshend House, built in 1879, now privately-owned and boasting the Blue Plaque conservation award. It was once the home of Jesse White, who was the niece of Samuel White, the local shipbuilder. In 1864 Jesse married Signor Mario, a member of Garibaldi's staff in Italy. Jesse went to Italy with her husband, and established herself as a heroine when she rode into battle with Garibaldi.

# THE PARADE

THE MARINE HOTEL 1890 26187

During the 17th century, smuggling around the coast of Britain became a highly lucrative trade, and could be just as vicious as it sometimes is today. Most of the islanders at that time were extremely poor, and like the inhabitants of other coastal areas saw smuggling as a way of augmenting their poverty-stricken existence. Running battles between the customs men and the smugglers were common. In 1777 a newly-appointed Collector of Customs, William Arnold, arrived to take up his post at Cowes. Since the building of the two castles in the reign of Henry VIII, prevention of smuggling in the coastal waters of the Island had been under the direction of the Customs. However, William Arnold was the first to be officially appointed as Collector of Customs. His task was overwhelming, for most of the Island was in league with the smugglers to one degree or another.

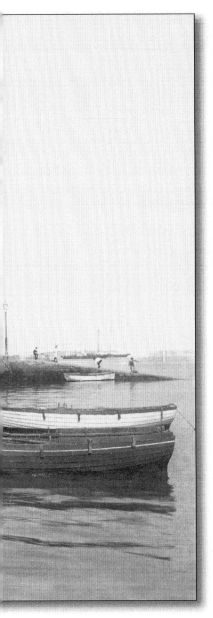

The Marine Hotel 1897  40369

The Parade 1908  60492

The donkey and cart standing outside the hotel would now be replaced by automobiles.
A yachting agency advertises itself on the left-hand side of the house by the Royal Marine
Hotel. The twin turrets on the seaward side of the Parade led to the pier; they are no longer
there, although today there are still numerous seats on which to rest. The elegant style of the
Edwardian black and white outfits give the Parade a graceful atmosphere.

### THE PARADE 1913 66311

The stateliness of the Royal Marine Hotel can be clearly seen here. Although women wear hats today, they are not usually as stylish as the black one with the veil that the lady on the bench is wearing. However, looking out to sea through binoculars is still a popular pastime. The benches are much smaller today. This scene seems so tranquil, yet the First World War was only months away.

# COWES

A little further along the road stands Mursell's Globe Hotel (26187, left, page 18), which was established by 1847. Today, having been refurbished in May 2001, it is an attractive restaurant called the Globe. Nearby stands the Royal Marine Hotel (26187, centre, and 40369, page 14). Both the Globe and Royal Marine Hotels were damaged by a freak whirlwind which hit Cowes on 28 September 1876. The buildings between the hotels are now privately-owned apartments.

The Royal Marine Hotel, now Marine Court, was one of the first hotels on the Island, dating from the 1830s. Its elegant iron balustrades have gone; no longer a hotel, it has become offices and flats. However, as the Royal Marine Hotel, it was most fashionable throughout the 19th century, entertaining wealthy and international guests. Indeed, Napoleon III of France stayed there in 1871 following his exile. Since the stone balustrade was built, boats can no longer be pulled right up to the Parade.

Next to Marine Court is a small building which houses a Model Railway Exhibition. Here too is an arc-shaped public shelter, and on its walls there are plaques which commemorate both history and tragedy. In the winter of 1633, two ships, the 'Ark' and the 'Dove', sailed from London to Maryland to establish a settlement under the King's Charter. The ships stopped at the port of Cowes to replenish their supplies and to take fresh water on board before their harrowing journey. Two plaques mark the 300th and 350th anniversaries of that voyage. Other plaques illustrate the heroism of our French and Polish allies during the Second World War and mark the bombing of Cowes on the night of 4-5 May 1942.

### THE GLOSTER HOTEL 1897 40370

The Gloster Hotel was the original home of the Royal Yacht Squadron in Cowes before it moved to the Castle; it stood at the far end of the Parade, next to the Victorian terrace. This elegant Victorian hotel with its iron railings and steps leading to the Parade has also been demolished since the Second World War. Almost on the same spot now stand the more modern Gloster Apartments.

### FROM THE PIER 1908 60494

At one time, elegant Victorian terraced houses, which were built between 1835 and 1857, graced the Parade. Apart from the last two terraced houses, these were demolished in the 1930s. In their place the Osborne Court apartments were built in Art Deco style just before the Second World War; they were used as a naval base during the war. Almost next door is the Royal London Yacht Club, which was formed in London in 1878. Part of this classical building was the home of Dr Hoffmeister, surgeon to Queen Victoria. The circular ornate railings on the Parade (foreground) were later removed.

### VIEW FROM THE PIER 1927 80463

A little higher up on a hill, peeping over the top of the Royal Marine Restaurant (far right) is the Trinity Theatre, which today houses the Cowes Amateur Operatic and Dramatic Society. The foundation stone for this theatre was laid in 1914. The Royal Marine Restaurant, next to the Royal Marine hotel, has been replaced by shops.

LEFT: VIEW FROM THE PIER 1927 80464

At the end of the Parade, behind the trees on the right, stands the Castle, the home of the Royal Yacht Squadron. Almost opposite today is the Royal Corinthian Yacht Club, another well-established club. It is here that a dog named Oscar is buried in the garden. Oscar was once a feature of the High Street as he lay outside Pascal Atkey's chandler's shop.

BELOW LEFT: VIEW FROM THE PIER 1933 85894

The ornate circular iron railings attached to the balustrade were replaced by a set of public toilets that stood on the Parade, but were removed after the Second World War. The crowd hugging the balustrade suggests that there must have been either a yacht race taking place or that persons of eminence were arriving at the Royal Yacht Squadron.

BELOW: THE PARADE C1955 C173010

A more casual style of dress had become popular by the 1950s. Motor bikes were a common feature of the Parade, and the number of cars was growing. Electric lights had replaced the gas lamps earlier in the century. Today, excursions can be taken by boat from the Parade during the summer months.

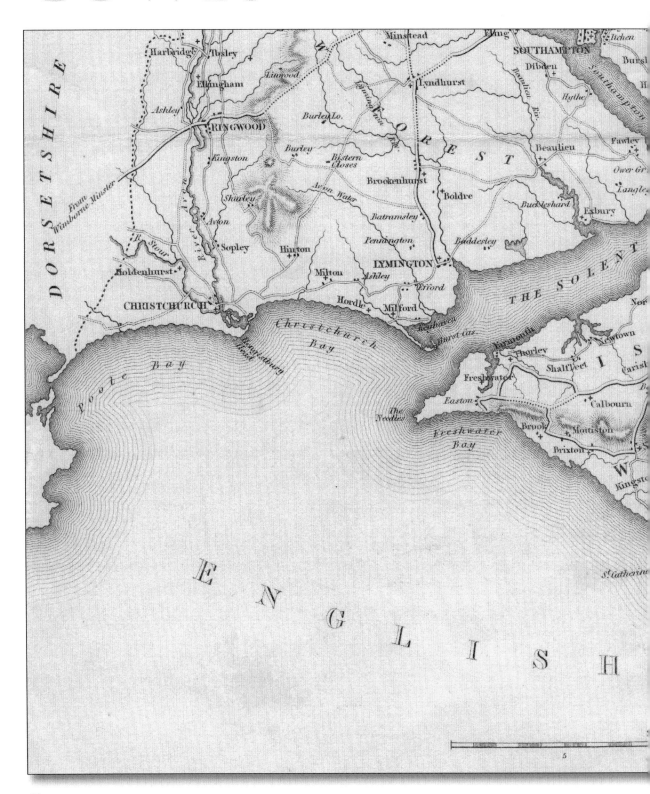

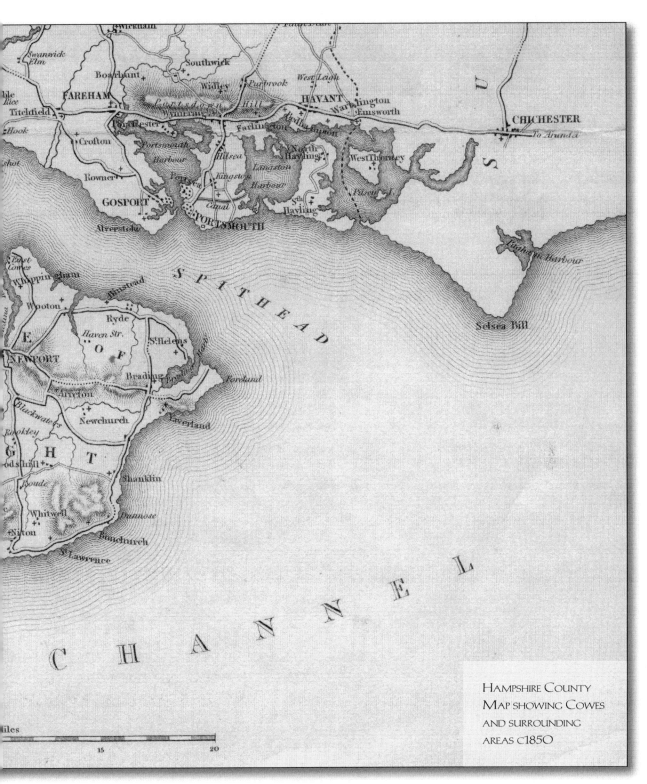

HAMPSHIRE COUNTY
MAP SHOWING COWES
AND SURROUNDING
AREAS c1850

# PIERS AND SAILING

By the middle of the 19th century, the railway system was expanding in all directions from London throughout the British Isles. This enabled people to travel quickly and easily to the south coast. The Isle of Wight was a happy beneficiary of the golden age of steam and rail, and quickly became a favoured holiday resort, especially for those living in London.

Today, when speed is everything, the fast ferry service is a perfectly normal mode of travel to and from the Island. However, it was difficult to reach the Island during the early years of its history. All that changed with the opening in 1840 of the London and South Western railway. For the first time, people could travel from London to Southampton in three hours, and then take an hour's trip across the Solent to England's Garden Isle.

By then, six steamers a day were making the return crossing from Southampton to the Island. The combination of regular trains and steam packets made the Isle of Wight accessible to all. Moreover, by the latter half of the 19th century, the Isle of Wight was becoming highly recommended as a health resort by the most eminent doctors in the land.

ABOVE:
### THE ROYAL YACHT SQUADRON 1923 74746

The popularity of watching visitors arrive and depart from
the landing stage by the Royal Yacht Squadron, or merely
waiting for the races to start, has never waned. The platform
with its striped awning is a feature of the Royal Yacht
Squadron.

LEFT: VICTORIA PIER 1908 60491

This imposing view of the harbour, and East Cowes on the
other side of the River Medina, acts as a backdrop to the new
Victoria Pier. The hackney carriages waiting for their fares,
and the numerous seats on the Parade, give the air of an
established seaside town.

### THE REGATTA 1903 50797B

The Pier, with its twin turrets at the entrance, was built in 1901 by the local council at a cost of £10,500, partly to attract business from the many pleasure steamers that were ploughing the Solent. From the seaward end of the pier there were excellent views of the harbour, passing ships, yacht racing, and regattas. The Pier was in use during the Second World War, but was demolished shortly after.

# PIERS AND SAILING

### WATCHING THE RACING 1933 85896

The crowds standing near the Pier show how popular yacht racing has always been. The style of clothes had changed drastically over the previous ten years from long skirts to shorter dresses. All the liners passing through the Solent could be seen from the Pier. The greatest liner of them all, the 'Queen Mary', with its three funnels, was a regular sight across the waters off Cowes Roads, as were the pilot boats ploughing to and fro in the Solent (C173012, page 34). The public toilets (behind the coach in C173012) replaced the iron railings, but were later demolished. By the 1950s, coaches were a regular feature along the water-front.

# PIERS AND SAILING

By 1824 it was becoming fashionable to be seen walking along the newly constructed Parade at Cowes, later the Victoria Parade. The adjoining Victoria Pier opened in 1902. The Victorians became great advocates of the delights of sea-bathing and chose Cowes as one of their favourite holiday resorts. Although there were several bathing machines at Cowes, in which people could undress and enter the sea in privacy, the shoreline is steep and the machines had to be lowered by means of a windlass until they reached the water.

The home at the water's edge of Uffa Fox, master yachtsman and designer, could be seen from the Pier. Uffa, as he was known to all, conceived, designed and built the airborne lifeboat at Cowes during the Second World War. He was enormously proud of his invention, and without doubt many airmen in the latter part of the war owed their lives to the brilliance and tenacity of Uffa Fox.

Cowes has a further claim to fame, for it was the local landowner, businessman and entrepreneur George Ward who started the Cowes to Southampton steam packet service in 1820. By 1824 he provided a round-the-Island trip as a passenger service. The voyage lasted six to seven hours, and the fare was just 25p.

LEFT: VICTORIA PIER 1923 74750

The fluttering Daily Mail sign shows that the Pier was used for advertisements. Steam boats at the boarding point by the Pier give some idea of the popularity of these vessels during the summer months. Shelters were available on the Pier for people to sit in, out of the sun or rain, and children often fished from the Pier.

BELOW LEFT: THE QUEEN MARY C1950 C173012

BELOW RIGHT: THE OLD PIER C1950 C173011

The old Pier, shortly before it was taken down, has a forlorn air about it. Although Dawson's souvenirs are being sold from one of its turrets, the 'no admittance' sign on the Pier sadly marks its imminent demise, along with its imposing twin turrets.

# PIERS AND SAILING

ABOVE: THE 'QUEEN MARY' c1955  C173004

The 'Queen Mary' often drew the crowds as she proudly made her way up the Solent - note the numbers of people and parked cars in C173004. The lorry almost hides the red telephone box standing on the Parade. The 'Queen Elizabeth', which we see passing Cowes on her way to berth at Southampton in C173017, is easily distinguishable from the 'Queen Mary' by her two funnels. Both ships were in service at the same time. This stretch of water has seen the departure of many famous vessels which subsequently led to historical events. These include Henry V's expedition to Harfleur and Nelson's 'Victory' sailing off to fight the French, as well as the D-Day invasion fleet.

BELOW: THE 'QUEEN ELIZABETH' c1955  C173017

# THE ROYAL YACHT SQUADRON

Henry VIII built forts as part of his coastal defences, in order to protect his merchant ships from attack by the French and Spanish, and also to protect his treasured dockyard at Portsmouth. His forts at Cowes helped protect the Isle of Wight as well as the immediate waterfront. Although the fort at Cowes is one of the oldest continuously occupied castles in English maritime history, remaining in military occupation for three centuries, not once have its guns been fired, either against an enemy or in the battles against the smugglers.

The roots of Cowes' importance as a premier yacht-racing haven began in the 18th century. During the first year of the American War of Independence in 1776, there was a yacht race at Cowes. The colonists had allied with the French in America; England now felt threatened by the French across the Channel and in America, so consequently only naval vessels were allowed to participate in the race. These vessels were based at West Cowes Castle, as it was then known.

In 1815, a club was founded in London at the Thatched House Tavern by 42 gentlemen engaged in salt-water yachting. In 1817 the Prince Regent joined the club, and on his ascent to the throne as George IV in 1820, the club became the Royal Yacht Club. The club made its first headquarters at the Medina hotel in East Cowes. In 1825, the club chose a house that later became the Gloster Hotel on the Parade at Cowes as its base and Cowes' yachting fame was sealed.

THE ROYAL YACHT SQUADRON CLUB HOUSE 1892  31401

Of all the clubs in the world, one of the most prestigious is the Royal Yacht Squadron at Cowes. Just as prestigious in its own right is its clubhouse, a castle, originally built by Henry VIII in 1539. The castle was one of two forts, one at East Cowes and one at Cowes. The East Cowes fort has completely disappeared.

# THE ROYAL YACHT SQUADRON

ABOVE: THE ROYAL YACHT SQUADRON c1955  C173024

The skill of island masons can be seen in the more recent additions to the Castle. A fence now hides the short castellated turret of the lodge on the road leading away from the castle. The viewing platform, with its striped awning, gives a clear view of the Solent for the club's members and guests. It is also where the computers are kept for collating races. There is a private landing place for members of the Royal Yacht Squadron and officers engaged on Her Majesty's Service.

RIGHT: THE 'VECTA' c1955  C173038

FAR RIGHT: THE ROYAL YACHT SQUADRON 1908  60495

# THE ROYAL YACHT SQUADRON

In 1826, there was a race between several yachts for a gold cup. Barring years of war, regattas and racing have continued until the present day.

The title of 'The Royal Yacht Squadron' was bestowed on the club by King William IV in 1833 as a mark of his 'approval of the institution as of national utility.' In 1858 the last captain of the castle died, and the club was allowed to take up residence there. Since then, it has had a long line of royal patronage, including Prince Philip. The club has become a world premier yachting club.

The battlements and lower parts of the castle are the original building, which were completed by Island masons using materials from stone quarries at Binstead on the Isle of Wight. The castle's walls and foundations frequently needed repairing because the foundations were so close to the sea. The footpath in front of the castle has not changed at all.

In photograph C173038 we can see the steam boat 'Vecta' making her way to the harbour. We can also see some of the 22 brass guns mounted in front of the castle; two were stolen on different occasions in the past, but they have been replaced. The originals came from William IV's yacht, the 'Royal Adelaide'. There is a warning sign posted on the path outside the Royal Yacht Squadron that states that a starting cannon may fire at any time! A particularly resounding shot was fired at the Jubilee Event of the Americas Cup in 2001. The vessels of members are privileged to fly the White Ensign of the Royal Navy; the Royal Yacht Squadron is the only club allowed to do so. The castle was used in the Second World War for planning of operations for the Normandy landing.

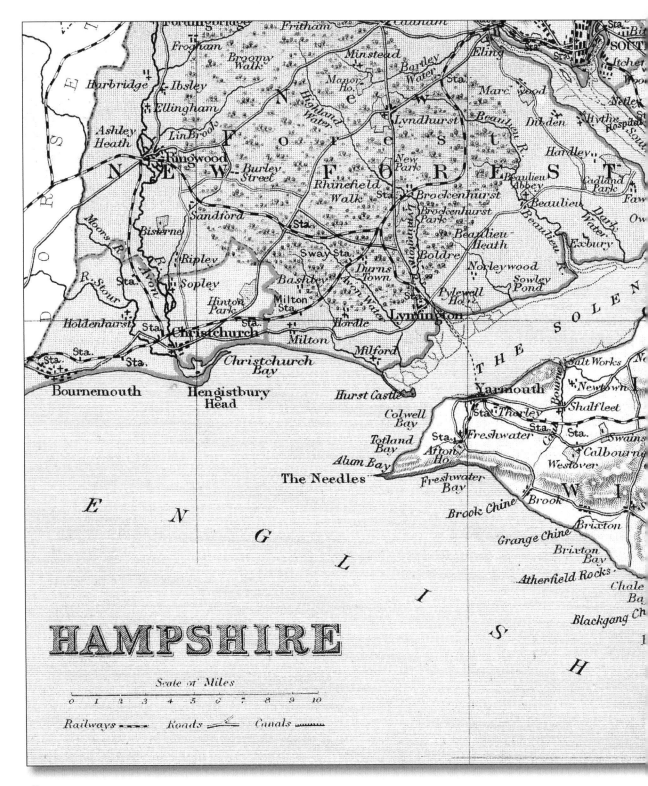

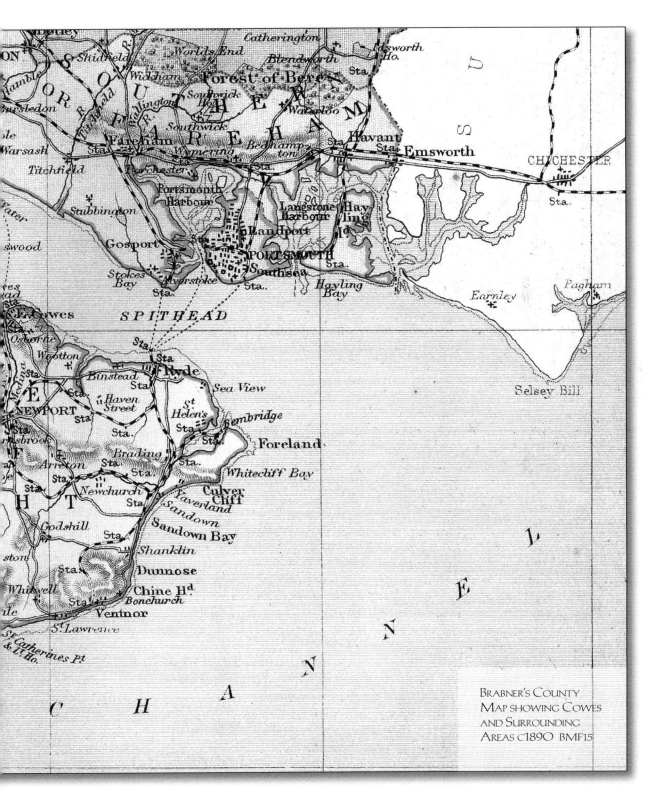

Brabner's County Map showing Cowes and Surrounding Areas c1890 BMF15

Next door to the Castle is Grantham Court, a newly-developed block of luxury apartments, built on the site of Grantham House. Originally home of members of the Robert Stephenson family, it later became a hotel. Robert Stephenson helped to open up the whole of England with the railway network. George Stephenson bought the two-acre Green (66317, below) alongside the building.

In 1864, George Stephenson gave the Green to the town to celebrate the marriage of the Prince of Wales (later Edward VII) to Princess Alexandra of Denmark. He also donated the bandstand, which was situated where the large round bush now stands, and provided uniforms for the Cowes Town Band. The occasion was celebrated in great style, with a large procession through the town, headed by a band. In the evening the choir and band dined in a marquee erected on the beach, whilst a dinner for townspeople took place in the Town Hall (which was bombed in the Second World War).

The road behind the Green is called Queen's Road. Here the nouveau riche Victorian industrialists bought land and built their spacious and elegant villas, often as second homes; Cowes was becoming a socially upwardly-mobile town. Some people would rent these villas out during the yachting season. Edward VII stayed at Saffa, a semi-detached elegant home of that period, on Queen's Road.

Away from the Castle, at the far end of the Green and the Esplanade, is Egypt Point. One explanation of the origin of the name is that the area was once a gypsy encampment. Gypsies were formerly known as Egyptians, since it was assumed that Egypt was their place of origin; gypsies, who had travelled from Dorset, were known to have been living near Gurnard since 1676.

THE GREEN AND THE SANDS 1913 66317

The Green 1890 26188

The Green, The Umbrella Tree 1913 66314

Towards the end of the Green, leading to the town, there is a large weeping ash known locally as the Umbrella Tree, which was planted by William Bilk in 1790. This was said to be a favourite place for courting couples.

### THE GREEN 1908 60499

Bathing was encouraged and these children, fully-clothed in their Edwardian outfits and hats, are paddling in the sea; but the coast shelves steeply here, which makes swimming difficult.

# THE ESPLANADE

THE HOLMWOOD HOTEL C1960  C173068

As we leave Egypt Point and go towards the town on Queen's Road we arrive at the New Holmwood Hotel, now a Best Western hotel, with an elegant blue-canopied entrance. Holmwood House was built in 1872 by Mr Charles Maw, head of the pharmaceutical firm known for babies' bottles, teats and other nursery equipment. His home was graced by a number of distinguished visitors during this period as, along with his neighbours, he rented his home to continental royalty.

THE ESPLANADE 1933 85897

Until recently, Egypt Point light was a navigational homing light for ships sailing from the west and making their way towards Southampton or Portsmouth. A large statue of a lion overlooking the Solent was erected by the West Cowes Board of Health in 1894. This was a favourite place for Queen Victoria and Prince Albert to stroll to watch the sunsets. Behind the Point stands Egypt House, owned by one of the descendants of the Ward family.

Before 1914, when the devastation of war was to sweep across Europe, Cowes was noted as a gathering place of crowned heads of state; this was owing to the rise in popularity of the yachting world and the royal estate at Osborne. Many would stay in homes along Queens Road, or would come to walk or enjoy the parties and regattas that took place.

In the history of the New Holmwood Hotel (C173068), Mr Denys Maw said that his grandfather's tenants occasionally included the Prince and Princess of Liechtenstein. Attending their extravagant parties was their German kinsman Kaiser Wilhelm II, who was an established yacht-racer. His cousin Edward VII would sometimes accompany him. Edward VII liked the idea of a post-box adorned with his cipher. He had one installed on the wall outside Holmwood in 1903, to match the one at the corner of Mornington Road and Queens Road bearing his mother's royal cipher.

Two white gate-posts stand at the end of a gravel drive leading to a white house called Beaulieu House at 47 Queens Road; here the Emperor Napoleon III and Empress Eugenie stayed when they were released from captivity after the Franco-Prussian War. Further along

# THE ESPLANADE

### LOWER GREEN 1913 66316

Opposite the small wood on the Lower Green there used to be a pavilion. Now in its place there is a modern ice cream kiosk and refreshment stand. The small wood was donated by ex-Wrens who were stationed at HMS Vectis.

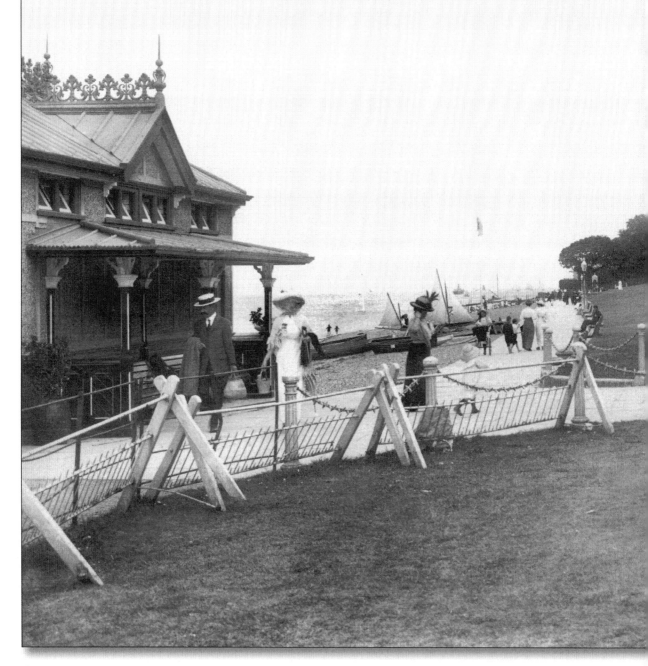

# THE ESPLANADE

the road towards the town is Rosetta Cottage, 57 Queens Road, a cream-coloured house with a castellated porch, now belonging to the National Trust. Before the road was built, this cottage was on the beach and was a rope maker's cottage. It is believed that ropes had been made here since the time of the Battle of Trafalgar. It is said that it was on the lawn of this garden that Lord Randolph Churchill proposed to Jennie Jerome. It was in the vicinity of Holmwood in the summer of 1874 that he had met Jennie Jerome for the second time; she was to become his wife, and they would be the parents of Winston Churchill. The engagement was announced at a party at Egypt House, and Queen Victoria attended.

In Victorian times a row of bathing machines stood along the shore line, waiting for their intrepid bathers. It was very close to here that Flora, a statue depicting the Roman goddess of flowers, was originally situated. It can now be seen at Northwood House.

Towards the seafront stands a Victorian drinking fountain (centre of 31399, page 52), which has been described as a sugar-icing fantasy in iron. Its classical design is highly decorative, and it was a public amenity in Victorian times. The fountain has recently been redecorated and restored to its former glory. The two public shelters on either side of the sugar fountain (centre of C173051, page 54) are still there today. In the distance we can see a small ice-cream kiosk where the Edwardian pavilion once stood, and where the modern refreshment building is now.

Just above the Royal Yacht Squadron, nestling into the hillside, is Holy Trinity Church (60498, page 53). It is known as the yachtsmen's church and the vicar is usually chaplain to the Royal Yacht Squadron. A service is held each year at the start of Cowes week and Prince Philip often reads the lesson. The church of yellow gault brick was built in 1832 at a cost of £6,687; it was consecrated on Midsummer's Day as 'the church on Cowes foreshore for sailors and seafarers'. It has a magnificent organ, rebuilt and paid for by the Beaverbrook Foundation. The church has been linked with the Royal Yacht Squadron since the mid 19th century.

The garden and terrace were laid out as a serene reminder of those who perished in the Fastnet Race in August 1979. The memorial stone to this very sad incident was quarried from the Fastnet Rock. The house next to the church, Guiness House, was built of the same yellow gault brick and was once occupied by Emma, Lady Hamilton.

## THE GREEN 1923  74751

Looking out to sea, the gathered crowd gazes at all kinds of vessels on the Solent. It is easy to visualise the activity that took place in these waters less than twenty years later, during the Second World War, when little boats crossed the Channel to help rescue the soldiers who were trapped at Dunkirk after the fall of France in 1940. In June 1944, this part of the Solent was crowded with landing craft and supply ships, which were sheltered and protected in these waters ready for the Normandy landings.

# THE ESPLANADE

A fortune was made in the City by the Ward family of Northwood House (C173029, page 56) who built up a property empire and were great benefactors to Cowes and other parts of the Island. They were also known for their lavish entertaining, and during Cowes regatta week Northwood House became a centre for wealthy socialites.

Facing the Solent, under the central portion of the house, is a Latin inscription, written by George Henry Ward to his mother (C173029, page 56); the translation is 'A son dedicates this house to the honoured name of his mother of outstanding merit'. To the left of this portion of the house and built into an alcove is the statue of Flora which once graced the Green overlooking the Esplanade. It was re-discovered and re-erected by local children at Lovelace Primary School, and was restored to the townsfolk on 3 May 1980. To the left of the statue, on a green slope, is the modern cenotaph memorial to the residents of Cowes who lost their lives in the two world wars. A memorial used to stand in the High Street at the bottom of Market Hill, but it was damaged in air raids in the Second World War and re-erected as a memorial to those who lost their lives in both wars.

Northwood House has seen many changes. It was a home for Benedictine nuns expelled from France in 1901, and the path which now runs above the tennis courts is still known as Nuns' Walk. The house was used by the Red Cross as a hospital in both world wars.

THE GREEN 1892 31399

HOLY TRINITY CHURCH 1908 60498

THE GREEN C1960 C173051

A casualty station was set up there during the air raids on Cowes on the night of 4 and 5 May 1942. In 1929, the house was given to Cowes by the Ward family, and is now used for office space and functions by the Medina Borough Council. The grounds are open to the public and delightful to walk through.

Here, too, by the house, is St Mary's Parish Church. This was founded in 1657 on land given by a supporter of Oliver Cromwell, but since that time much of the church has been rebuilt. Charles Wesley preached here in 1735 when his boat was delayed in the Cowes Roads on his way to Georgia. On the south wall of the church there is a plaque to Thomas Arnold, the famous headmaster of Rugby School, who was baptized at St Mary's.

Cowes has other interesting churches including the Roman Catholic Church in Terminus Road. Built in 1796, the church has a 16th-century painting, said to be the work of Allesandro da Messina, representing the death of the Virgin Mary.

NORTHWOOD HOUSE C1955 C173029

Northwood House, set in Northwood Park, is approachable by both road and path, but it is a steep climb either way. At the end of the 18th century, George Ward bought the manor of Northwood. Northwood House, previously known as Bellevue House, was rebuilt between 1837 and 1838 for his son George Henry Ward. An extra wing was added in 1840. The house was reputed to be designed by John Nash, although it was not built until three years after Nash's death. It has a classical exterior and an Egyptian and Etruscan interior.

In Bath Road (80465, page 66 and C173001, page 58) is the Solent Ice Cream shop, the back of the Model Railway Exhibition, and Kendall's Fine Art shop - its owner was Kenneth Kendall, once a BBC newsreader. On the opposite side of the road is the Regatta Centre and Skandia Life office, showing lists of the regattas taking place. The characterful tea shop building at the bottom of the road is still there (80465, left), but it now houses a dentist's office. There is also an unclaimed property shop here.

Further up the street on the right hand side is Beken and Son, photographers, not to be confused with Beken, the marine photographers, on the Birmingham Road. The shop stands in front of the Trinity Theatre. Here too is the Cowes Operatic and Dramatic

Society charity shop; the Society has the freehold ownership of the theatre. A Thai restaurant and another Kendall's art shop lead up the street.

At one time, the greengrocer's business of Mrs Ash, 3l Bath Road, was the last shop before entering the High Street, but now it is the Watch House Barn Coffee Shop and Restaurant. Opposite, on the corner, is the Charles Dickens Book shop; next door to that, on the right, is Flagstaff Antiques and Ian Rose Marine Paintings. The Union Inn, one of the oldest inns in Cowes, still stands at the top of the High Street. On the corner of Watch House Lane is the office of the Island Sailing Club.

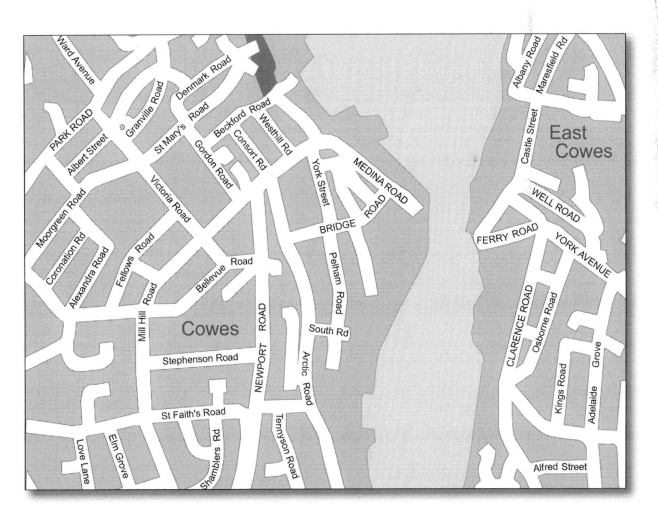

COWES

BATH ROAD c1955 C173001

HIGH STREET c1955 C173002

OLD HOUSES 1927
80465

We are at the bottom
of Bath Road, which
leads onto the Parade.
The buildings look
much the same today
as they have done for
a long time, although
shops have come
and gone. This was
one of the earliest
parts of Cowes to be
developed after the
boom in the tourist
trade in the early 19th
century. The Pavilion
Hotel is no longer
there; the back of the
arc-shaped public
shelter on the Parade
stands in its place.

61

# THE TOWN

Facing the town, on the right-hand side of the High Street, is Benzie's, the nautical jeweller's shop, world-famous for its original jewellery designed for lady and gentlemen yachtsmen. The shop is the official jewellers to the Americas Cup Jubilee. There is an observation tower on top of the shop, and in Victorian times at 12 noon precisely it received a time signal from Greenwich via Portsmouth Town Hall. It was for many years the chief time-keeper for the Royal Navy in the East Solent, and has many Royal Warrants. Opposite Benzie's is the Americas Cup Jubilee Office, a waterside properties agent's office and the old Lloyds Bank building, which has now been renovated.

Hewitts once described itself as a 'Yachting, Export and Family Grocers, Wine, Spirit, Ale and Provision Merchant'. This shop had a large warehouse at the back, which went down to the water's edge, and it was a three-storey building until it was bombed in 1942. The warehouse was later converted into a house for Uffa Fox. As a grocer's shop, Hewitts held a warrant to blend teas for Queen Victoria. The Galleries Segui clothes shop is next door to Hewitts. Green's restaurant on the left, below, is no longer there, but the private apartments next door to Green's still exist.

Along the High Street on the left is the Max Aitken Museum, containing mementoes from the years he spent in Cowes. The Royal Ocean Club also uses this building as an office. Next door is the Prospect, which once belonged to the family of Ratsey and Lapthorn the sailmakers; now part of it is used by the Max Aitken Museum.

Here too is the Cowes Royal British Legion, HSBC Bank and the old Mew Langton building, today a clothes shop. This building extends back to the waterfront, and was used as a brewery depot. The beer came on barges by water and was taken to various inns by dray-horse. Almost directly opposite is the Ocean World clothing shop, earlier Morgan and Sons. It is the aim of many shop owners to gain the royal warrant, and thus supply goods to the royal family; Morgan & Sons was one such shop. They were the originators of the yachtsman's uniform of navy blazer, flannel trousers and peaked cap. They outfitted the crews of about 100 yachts a year.

On the opposite side of the High Street, at the bottom of Sun Hill, there is a large Georgian house with a Sun Insurance fire sign on the front. Almost opposite is the Three Crowns public house. The inn was originally built in the late 17th century, and is reputed to be haunted.

ABOVE: HIGH STREET C1965 C173082

LEFT: HIGH STREET C 1965 C173081

Further down the road from Benzie's, on the left, is a Spar grocery shop with the sign of Hewitt and Son, Est 1790. Directly opposite on the corner are town-houses where the George Hotel once stood, until it was bombed in the Second World War, as was Cowes Town Hall. Here too stood the First World War memorial, shattered in the same raid, now re-erected at Northwood House. The Westminster Bank building still stands, but is now William Joyce's jewellery workshop. Next to the Westminster Bank building today are several shops, including clothing stores and a Stitch in Time.

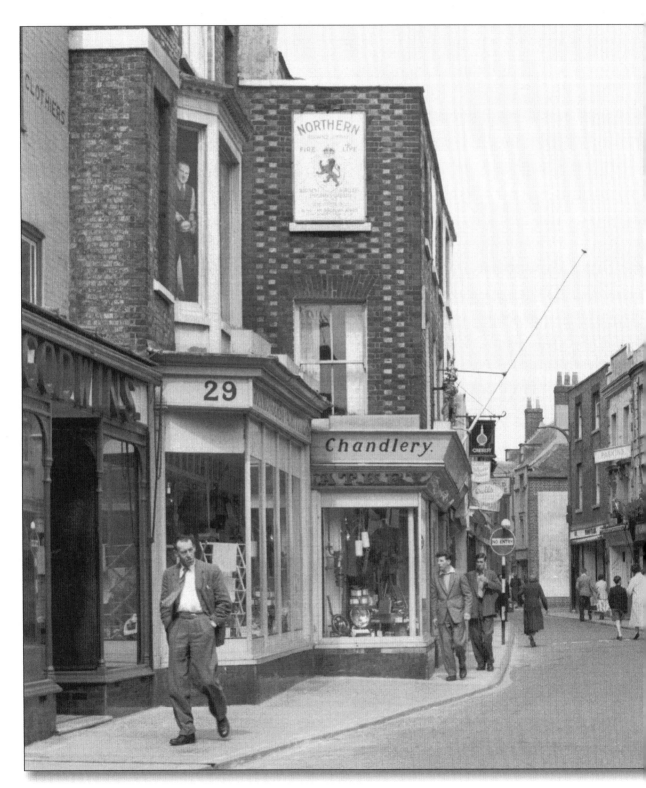

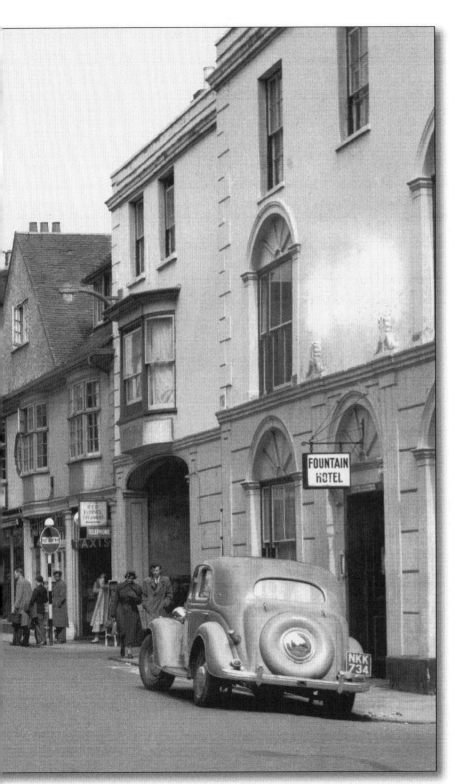

### HIGH STREET C1955 C173039

On the right side of the street is the Fountain Hotel, built in 1803 as a coaching inn. It owned all the buildings behind it, which were used for servants' quarters and stables. At one time practically every other building in this area was a public house. Coaches left for Newport and Ventnor from here. There is a high arch beside the hotel, leading to the Arcade. The hotel was once the very centre of town social events. Dancing took place here, and magic lantern shows were brought from London in the winter, a highly popular form of entertainment for townsfolk. Sad to say, the Fountain Hotel is now one of the few residential hotels in Cowes.

# THE TOWN

Along the High Street, on the seaward side where the road becomes narrow, is 92 High Street. This housed Woodyear and Sons, a drapery shop which once supplied linens to Queen Victoria at Osborne House, but now sells sport and leisure wear. The shop still has the original wooden counter. There are several shops, including a sailing store and Nationwide, before reaching the Arcade. Opposite the old Woodyear shop is 'tHat Shop', a curio shop, which used to be The Hat Shop.

Next door to the Fountain Hotel (C173039, page 65 and C173085, below) is the Vectis Tavern, dating from about 1590, and opposite, on the corner of Terminus Road, is the Pier View Inn. This area was known as the Town Square, where people could gather to watch Morris Men dancing and small firework displays. It was a popular drinking area for sailors whose ships were anchored in the harbour.

Opposite the Fountain Hotel is a shop very well known to many sailors, Pascal Atkeys, established in 1799 (on the left of C173085). Until fairly recently, Pascal Atkeys was owned by the Atkey family, a very old Island family. It was once much bigger, and included the clothing shop next door. It has the honour of being one of the oldest chandleries in the country, and is built of ships' timbers, which are still visible inside the store. There is a memorial seat to Oscar the dog, 1980-96, who used to sun himself on the pavement outside the shop and was noted by all who passed by. He is buried at the Royal Corinthian Yacht Club. To the right of Pascal Atkey's, opposite the Arcade, is the Southern Vectis Island bus transport centre. The service provided is much relied upon by islanders and visitors alike.

HIGH STREET c1965 C173085

By 1861, the Red Funnel Steamship Company had begun to operate from the Arcade (C173076, below), but the landing stage reaches far back into Cowes' history. After the Red Funnel Company began to ply its trade, the Arcade became alive with the noise of the fish markets held there and cattle waiting to be shipped to Southampton. All this activity took place amidst the horse-drawn carriages taking their passengers to the ticket office and the paddle steamers. Later, the carriages were replaced by cars and charabancs. Whilst car ferries no longer stop at the pontoon (they call at East Cowes), foot passengers can take a fast passenger service to Southampton.

The shop next door to Pittis & Son (C173086, page 71), on the right-hand side of the road as it narrows, is now White Stuff, and just beyond that is the Carphone Warehouse. Opposite, with slightly changed shop fronts, are Aqua Togs clothes and a fried chicken shop where once were Rileys and Kays. A little further up the High Street

is The Cut, on the right-hand side. This was where the village ended in the 18th century. Boots the chemist is on one corner, and a health shop is on the other, called Beken & Son, but it no longer belongs to the Beken family.

Past this, on the right-hand side, is the Anchor public house, built in 1704 and constructed of ships' timbers. It was then known as the Three Trumpeters and it later became the principal coaching inn of Cowes because of its ample room for stabling. At the top of the road stands Somerfield Stores. Just before the store on the left-hand side is Café Tiffins bar and restaurant. At the side there is an entrance to Cowes Yacht Haven on Marina Walk. The Cowes Town Waterfront Trust is a registered charity, dedicated to rejuvenating the waterfront of Cowes. The Yacht Haven is being refurbished, helped by a grant by the EEC; there will be new facilities for the sailors, and room for 200 yachts to anchor.

## FOUNTAIN ARCADE C1965 C173076

Next to the Fountain Hotel is an archway leading to the Fountain Arcade. On one side of the Arcade is a covered walkway where there are shops and the Tourist Information Centre. At the end of the Arcade is the Red Funnel ticket office, which has pictures of steam packets and ships on the walls inside. The fast ferry passenger service for Southampton leaves from here.

THE PIER 1893 32838

# EAST MEETS WEST

ABOVE: HIGH STREET C1965  C173087

The High Street leads to Shooters Hill, which was once a very swampy area. The buildings are shaped here to follow the curve of the road. The first shop on the right is now a florist. Morgans, 'Complete House Furnishers', has become the Alamo restaurant and bar. Opposite from the bottom of the hill up, are Chiverton's Newsagents, Bath Travel, an Italian restaurant and a pet supplies shop.

ABOVE RIGHT: HIGH STREET C1955  C173046

Opposite the Vectis Tavern is Terminus Road, where the Newport to Cowes Railway Company built its station in 1862. The last train from Cowes ran in 1966, and all traces of the station have disappeared. Past the Vectis Tavern was the National Provincial Bank. The Commercial Inn still stands, but is now Murrays Seafood Restaurant, favoured by many yachtsmen. Next door to Murrays was Olivers' shoe shop, today T M Taylor & Sons, jewellers. Their previous shop is now the Shoreline Picture Gallery; next door is the Mantrap boutique.

BELOW RIGHT: HIGH STREET C1965  C173086

# EAST MEETS WEST

At the top of the High Street on the right is the Cowes Advertiser office, but just before that is the NSPCC charity shop. It was once Shergold's grocery, and still has beautiful tiles on the walls. Next door to that is Joliffe's shoe shop, established 1853, now closed, which has a handsome decorated tiled and stained glass front.

On the right in Beckford Road is the public library and the Maritime Museum. The Museum displays paintings, logbooks, model ships, and yacht designs by Uffa Fox, and is a sailor's haven. Uffa used the carriageway of the old 1896 Floating Bridge as his workshop. At the top of Shooters Hill there is a sign-post. To the left

of the sign-post between the buildings can be seen a lovely view of the harbour and the boats of the Yacht Haven.

On the same side of the road as the chemist's shop was Alexander Hall, now Alexander House (the pedimented building). This was a public hall where the people of Cowes watched theatre groups and attended dances. The theatre group has now transferred to the Trinity Theatre. Opposite Alexander House was once the Royal Cinema. There too is Beken, the world famous photographers, with the sign over the door 'By appointment to HRH the Duke of Edinburgh - Marine Photographers'.

BIRMINGHAM ROAD C1965 C173088

Shooters Hill leads to Birmingham Road. Baileys, on the corner of Beckford Road, is now Earth Wind Water and Offshore Sports. On the left in the three-storey brick house is Beken & Son, the chemist, established in 1839 at Blenheim House. The shop was refronted in 1835 by Wyatt, the Victorian builder. The original 'by appointment' signs to Queen Victoria and the Prince of Wales can still be seen in Beken, the world-famous marine photographers, which is opposite.

West Cowes, From the Ferry c1955  C173008

The Floating Bridge 1913  66313

# COWES

## EAST MEETS WEST

Further down the road on the same side is the Methodist Church. Almost directly opposite is Westbourne House, where a plaque reveals that Thomas Arnold, the reforming headmaster of Rugby School, was born here on 13 June 1795. His son was Matthew Arnold, the poet and scholar. Thomas Arnold's father, William Arnold, was Collector of Customs; during his term of office on the Island, based at Cowes, he was indefatigable in rooting out the corruption of those under his command in the preventive force.

On the corner of Birmingham Road and Mill Hill is the police station. The road branches left, turning into Medina Road. On the left can be found the old Cowes boatbuilders, Clare Ludlow. The family firm built the 'Morning Cloud' yachts for former Prime Minister Edward Heath. Here too by the waters' edge is Shepards Wharf, the oldest quay in Cowes.

We come now to the end of Cowes, to the River Medina and to the chain link ferry (E139008, page 72). Looking from East Cowes, we see Point Cottages on the left. A little further along the road is the sailmaker's loft built for Henry VII's navy in 1543 - it now belongs to Ratsey and Lapthorn (Sailmakers) Ltd. This old stone building has stood the test of time. Here too are the offices of J Samuel White, the shipbuilders, a most famous firm, now in the hands of the County Council. Once warships were built in their yards, both in East Cowes and Cowes. The business, which was eventually to become known as J S White and Co Ltd, began as a small family boatbuilding business at Broadstairs in Kent; in 1802 Thomas White moved to East Cowes.

The ferry rights were originally granted to the Roberton family in 1720 by the Island Governor. They held the rights until 1859, when they sold out to the Cowes Ferry Company. The Cowes Ferry Company in turn sold the ferry rights to Red Funnel in 1868. From 1901, the East and West Cowes Councils took over the running of the Floating Bridge, and since 1972 the County Council has run it.

When Queen Victoria travelled on the Floating Bridge nobody else was allowed on board. At other times, it was crowded with horses as well as people (see 40368a). There are now plans for a road bridge over the River Medina, a little way upstream.

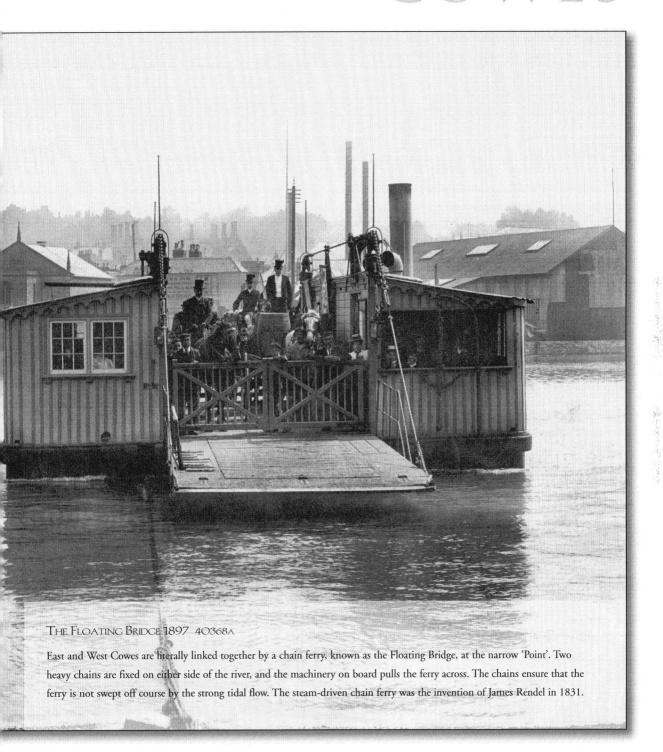

THE FLOATING BRIDGE 1897 40368A

East and West Cowes are literally linked together by a chain ferry, known as the Floating Bridge, at the narrow 'Point'. Two heavy chains are fixed on either side of the river, and the machinery on board pulls the ferry across. The chains ensure that the ferry is not swept off course by the strong tidal flow. The steam-driven chain ferry was the invention of James Rendel in 1831.

ORDNANCE SURVEY
MAP SHOWING COWES
AND SURROUNDING
AREAS C1900

# EAST COWES

The River Medina, which separates East Cowes and Cowes, is navigable for six miles inland as far as Newport, the county town. East Cowes, unlike its twin across the river, is not known for its glamorous yachting scene. Instead, it is proud to boast a history of shipbuilding, and hovercraft and aeroplane construction and development. Large commercial vessels use the river, as well as many yachts. East Cowes was the country home of Queen Victoria and her family for over fifty years. Through its streets, frock-coated politicians passed, bearing papers concerning affairs of state that would affect the whole of the Empire.

J Samuel White (whose premises can be seen in E139004) built ships for the Royal Navy, including destroyers and submarines, in its shipyards in both East Cowes and Cowes. The firm built up a world-wide reputation, particularly under J Samuel White, and built ships for many of the world's navies, in particular the Polish destroyer 'Blyskawica', which helped to save Cowes when the town was heavily bombed on the night of 4 May 1942. It was a measure of the importance of White's that the Germans were trying to put them out of action. In E139004 too we see an updated version of the Floating Bridge.

Following the pioneering spirit of Moses Saunders, its founder, Saunders-Roe (E139005) became involved in helicopters and hovercraft in the 1950s. In 1960 Saunders-Roe became part of Westland Aircraft Ltd, and in 1966 it was renamed the British Hovercraft Corporation. The large door (E139005, background) was painted as a Union Jack to commemorate the Queen's Silver Jubilee in 1977. The firm of Saunders-Roe built lifeboats, and also Sir Malcolm Campbell's famous 'Bluebird', which broke the world speed record in 1936. Saunders pioneered flying boats with Sopwith and A V Roe, and the firm also produced seaplanes.

In time, the British Hovercraft Corporation took over the premises of Saunders-Roe, and today the premises belong to Westland Aerospace. The huge Union Flag, painted on its doors for Queen Elizabeth II's Silver Jubilee, remains there by request of the public. The SRN 1, the first hovercraft in the world, was built in East Cowes; it was launched on 11 June 1959.

### EAST COWES
### SAUNDERS-ROE
### SEAPLANE BASE c1955
### E139005

The firm was founded by Moses Saunders, a Surrey boatbuilder, in 1830, but it did not come to the Island until 1901. Samuel Saunders was one of the first people to put petrol engines in boats; being a pioneer, he became interested in aviation before the First World War. In 1928 the firm was renamed Saunders-Roe Ltd, when it was taken over by a consortium led by Alliott

### EAST COWES
### THE DOCKYARD c1955
### E139004

The Harbour c1960  C173061

# EAST COWES

Crossing over on the Floating Bridge from Cowes to East Cowes is like stepping back in time. This atmosphere can be felt as one walks to the town centre on York Avenue (E139058), the road that leads up to Osborne House. A number of seats on the pavement are there to give the traveller a moment to rest and gather his or her thoughts.

On the corner of Clarence Road and York Avenue is Watson, Bull and Porter, estate agents, once Godwins; facing them on the corner of York Avenue is Lloyds Pharmacy (E139058, centre), and opposite on York Avenue is a Somerfields supermarket. At the bottom of York Avenue is Castle Street. To the right, on both sides, is Westland Aerospace.

In 1895, the Liquid Fuel Engineering company (at the Columbine Yard, to the left in Castle Street) was building not only steam launches, but also steam cars - it was obviously an engineering company with great foresight. Then in 1906 Samuel Saunders bought the firm to create the Columbine Yard. The Columbine yard building has seen the construction of the Princess flying boats and hovercraft. Built in the early 1950s, the Princess was the biggest plane in the world at that time; only three were built. At the cross-roads of Marsefield Road by the harbour, the Victoria Barracks are on the right. They were built in 1872 to house troops to guard Queen Victoria when she was in residence at Osborne House.

On the Esplanade is a handsome terrace of coastguard cottages, built in 1881 (see 31402, page 85). By the 18th century, East Cowes was the customs post of the whole island, before the office moved to Cowes. Here, just before Cambridge Road, is the propeller belonging to HMS 'Cavalier'. Built in East Cowes by J S White in 1944, this ship was the fastest in the Royal Navy for 27 years. Beyond the propeller is an ornate Victorian drinking fountain. There are many seats here on which to sit and enjoy the beautiful view across the harbour to Cowes.

Here too is the Trinity House entrance, where there was once an elaborate gate to be used by Queen Victoria when she boarded her royal yacht. Trinity House looks after all the light houses and buoys around the coast of England and Wales.

Two public wells served the town in 1850. The water was often contaminated, and there was a severe typhoid epidemic in the 1850s. The average life expectancy in East Cowes in 1851 was just 25.8 years.

Osborne House (32830, page 86), Queen Victoria's country retreat, was purchased in 1845 with an estate of about 1,000 acres, along with the adjacent Barton Manor, which served as the home farm and housed the Queen's grooms. The old house was demolished; in its place, between 1845 and 1851, was erected an Italianate building, designed jointly by Prince Albert and Thomas Cubit. East Cowes' future as a tourist spot was assured.

The Pavilion was completed first. This portion contained the formal rooms: the drawing room, the dining room and also the billiard room. The private apartments on the first floor were more informal, and the household wing was completed in 1851. In front

HOVERCRAFT C1965 C173090

THE HARBOUR C1965 C173083

EAST COWES, YORK AVENUE C1955 E139058

On one side of York Avenue there is an umbrella tree. A little further up the road is the Liberal Club of East Cowes, dated 1914, and there too is the Town Hall, now a community centre. There is a second-hand furniture shop on the corner of Clarence Road, behind the umbrella tree. During Victoria's reign, the buildings along that side of Clarence Road were a barracks. On the other side of Clarence Road is the Heritage Centre.

# EAST COWES

of the house, there is a mock Renaissance terrace with fountains, all in keeping with the general design. At the far end of High Walk is the Swiss Cottage, given to the royal children, and a museum with the curios they collected. To Osborne's Council Rooms came eminent statesmen involved with the governance of the Empire. The Council Rooms have now been fitted with the original silk carpet which came from the Great Exhibition of 1851.

Prince Albert died in 1861 of typhoid; to Victoria this felt like a death-blow, as she was totally dependant upon her husband. He was an extremely efficient private and personal secretary to the Queen, and also a man of many interests. After a long mourning period, the Queen once again gave audience to her ministers.

In 1876 Queen Victoria became Empress of India. Although the Queen never visited India, she became fascinated by all things Indian. Indeed, in 1887 an Indian, Abdul Karim, went to Osborne; in time he became the Queen's personal Indian secretary, and taught her Hindustani.

Entering the Durbar Room at Osborne House (60585, page 86), is like changing continents. The Indian architecture and the rich embellishment of every surface from floor to ceiling transports the visitor to the world of India. The Indian symbolism of the decorations include Ganesa, the elephant god of good fortune, and the peacock over the chimney-piece. Over 500 hours were spent on producing the peacock alone. From Queen Victoria's Jubilees of 1887 and 1897 come the many detailed Indian objects on display. This room has now been beautifully refurbished, and exhibits the exquisite gifts given to Queen Victoria by the Indian people. Queen Victoria died on 22 January 1901.

Osborne House has been in the care of English Heritage since 1984. In the centenary year 2001, the dining room was refurbished and shows the table in the process of being laid for one of the family dinners.

Adjoining the Osborne Estate is Norris Castle, which was built for Lord Seymour in the 1790s. Queen Victoria was a regular visitor as a young girl with her mother. Here too is St Mildred's church, Whippenham, the site of a Saxon church, rebuilt by John Nash in 1804, and rebuilt again by 1862. It was the parish church for Osborne.

After Queen Victoria died, her son Edward VII gave Osborne House to the nation, as he had been unhappy there as a child. Later, two wings became a convalescent home for officers. However, the King kept Barton Manor and entertained there magnificently.

In 1909, his guest list included the entire Russian royal family, the Emperor of Germany and the King of Spain. During the time the Queen was at Osborne, the British Empire had expanded throughout the world; the Isle of Wight and East Cowes is part of that history.

The halcyon days for the royals and their wealthy visitors ended with the outbreak of the First World War, for Island life was immediately disrupted. All yachting ceased; the ferry service with the mainland was discontinued, and for the duration of the war the island was isolated.

Life was never quite the same again for the aristocratic families on the Island after the war. Cowes, however, recovered its popularity for yachting; apart from the Second World War, it has boomed through to this present time.

## The World's Oldest Sporting Trophy

The first international yacht race around the island took place 150 years ago. This was an event of unforseeable importance in yacht racing; it was without doubt one of the cornerstones on which a multi-million pound industry was built. The race came to be known world-wide as the Americas Cup. The New York Yacht Club challenged the Royal Yacht Squadron as part of the celebrations of the Great Exhibition of 1851. The schooner 'America' was sent across the Atlantic, and proceeded to beat all the English yachts in a race that lasted more than ten hours. Every attempt since that time by the English to win back the solid silver ewer has been unsuccessful.

A celebration of the race, together with the annual Cowes week, the Round the Island race, the Admirals Cup, the Fastnet race and many other regattas was part of the Jubilee Regatta of 2001, which filled the waters around Cowes with yachts, sailors and visitors from all over the world.

A FLYING BOAT C1955 C173016

The seaplane is in the Medina, lying off Trinity wharf, which is the other side of the long groyne sticking out into the harbour from the left. Back to Castle Road, towards the Floating Bridge, the Southampton, Isle of Wight and South of England Mail Steam Packet Public Ltd Co (the full name for Red Funnel), had a ferry terminal at East Cowes since 1861 on this site. The public slipway between the Red Funnel and Trinity House was once called Blood Bay by the locals, because butchers got rid of their offal into the sea here. This is now the Red Funnel office.

EAST COWES, THE COASTGUARD STATION 1892 31402

# EAST COWES

## OSBORNE HOUSE 1893 32830

'A place of one's own, quiet and retired', were Queen Victoria's words when she and Prince Albert were looking for a family retreat in the country. Queen Victoria had married Prince Albert of Saxe-Coburg in 1840. Their choice of homes was very grand, including Buckingham Palace, Windsor Castle and the Brighton Pavilion, and the royal couple felt in need of privacy away from the ceremonial courts. The Queen was no stranger to the Isle of Wight; she had visited it twice as a young girl with her widowed mother, and had formed a fondness for the Island.

## OSBORNE HOUSE, THE STATE APARTMENTS, THE INDIAN DURBAR ROOM 1908 60585

The Durbar Room was created in order to provide a state banqueting room. It was designed by Lockwood Kipling, father of Rudyard Kipling, and the principal craftsman was Bhai Ram Singh. The name 'Durbar' is derived from an Indian word meaning both a state reception and a hall for gatherings. Before the Durbar Room was built, important receptions had been held in marquees on the lawn. The Durbar Room was constructed between 1890-91.

# INDEX

# FRITH PRODUCTS & SERVICES

Francis Frith would doubtless be pleased to know that the pioneering publishing venture he started in 1860 still continues today. Over a hundred and forty years later, The Francis Frith Collection continues in the same innovative tradition and is now one of the foremost publishers of vintage photographs in the world. Some of the current activities include:

## INTERIOR DECORATION

Today Frith's photographs can be seen framed and as giant wall murals in thousands of pubs, restaurants, hotels, banks, retail stores and other public buildings throughout the country. In every case they enhance the unique local atmosphere of the places they depict and provide reminders of gentler days in an increasingly busy and frenetic world.

## PRODUCT PROMOTIONS

Frith products are used by many major companies to promote the sales of their own products or to reinforce their own history and heritage. Frith promotions have been used by Hovis bread, Courage beers, Scots Porage Oats, Colman's mustard, Cadbury's foods, Mellow Birds coffee, Dunhill pipe tobacco, Guinness, and Bulmer's Cider.

## GENEALOGY AND FAMILY HISTORY

As the interest in family history and roots grows world-wide, more and more people are turning to Frith's photographs of Great Britain for images of the towns, villages and streets where their ancestors lived; and, of course, photographs of the churches and chapels where their ancestors were christened, married and buried are an essential part of every genealogy tree and family album.

## FRITH PRODUCTS

All Frith photographs are available Framed or just as Mounted Prints and Posters (size 23 x 16 inches). These may be ordered from the address below. Other products available are- Address Books, Calendars, Jigsaws, Canvas Prints, Coasters, Notelets and local and prestige books.

## THE INTERNET

Already ninety thousand Frith photographs can be viewed and purchased on the internet through the Frith websites and a myriad of partner sites.

For more detailed information on Frith companies and products, look at this site:
www.francisfrith.com

See the complete list of Frith Books at: www.francisfrith.com
This web site is regularly updated with the latest list of publications from The Francis Frith Collection. If you wish to buy books relating to another part of the country that your local bookshop does not stock, you may purchase on-line.

*For further information, trade, or author enquiries please contact us at the address below:*
**The Francis Frith Collection, Frith's Barn, Teffont, Salisbury, Wiltshire, England SP3 5QP.**
Tel: +44 (0)1722 716 376  Fax: +44 (0)1722 716 881  Email: sales@francisfrith.co.uk

See Frith products on the internet at www.francisfrith.com

# FREE PRINT OF YOUR CHOICE

**Mounted Print**
*Overall size 14 x 11 inches (355 x 280mm)*

**Choose any Frith photograph in this book.**
Simply complete the Voucher opposite and return it with your remittance for £3.50 (to cover postage and handling) and we will print the photograph of your choice in SEPIA (size 11 x 8 inches) and supply it in a cream mount with a burgundy rule line (overall size 14 x 11 inches).
**Please note: aerial photographs and photographs with a reference number starting with a "Z" are not Frith photographs and cannot be supplied under this offer. Offer valid for delivery to one UK address only.**

**PLUS: Order additional Mounted Prints at HALF PRICE - £9.50 each** (normally £19.00)
If you would like to order more Frith prints from this book, possibly as gifts for friends and family, you can buy them at half price (with no additional postage and handling costs).

**PLUS: Have your Mounted Prints framed**
For an extra £18.00 per print you can have your mounted print(s) framed in an elegant polished wood and gilt moulding, overall size 16 x 13 inches (no additional postage and handling required).

---

**IMPORTANT!**

**These special prices are only available if you use this form to order. You must use the ORIGINAL VOUCHER on this page (no copies permitted). We can only despatch to one UK address. This offer cannot be combined with any other offer.**

---

*Send completed Voucher form to:*
**The Francis Frith Collection, Frith's Barn, Teffont, Salisbury, Wiltshire SP3 5QP**

# CHOOSE A PHOTOGRAPH FROM THIS BOOK

*Voucher* for **FREE** *and Reduced Price Frith Prints*

*Please do not photocopy this voucher. Only the original is valid, so please fill it in, cut it out and return it to us with your order.*

| Picture ref no | Page no | Qty | Mounted @ £9.50 | Framed + £18.00 | Total Cost £ |
|---|---|---|---|---|---|
| | | 1 | Free of charge* | £ | £ |
| | | | £9.50 | £ | £ |
| | | | £9.50 | £ | £ |
| | | | £9.50 | £ | £ |
| | | | £9.50 | £ | £ |
| | | | £9.50 | £ | £ |
| | | | * Post & handling | | £3.50 |
| | | | Total Order Cost | | £ |

*Please allow 28 days for delivery. Offer available to one UK address only*

Title of this book . . . . . . . . . . . . . . . . . . . . . . . . . . . . . .

I enclose a cheque/postal order for £ . . . . . . . . . . .
made payable to 'The Francis Frith Collection'

OR please debit my Mastercard / Visa / Maestro card, details below

Card Number:

Issue No (Maestro only):          Valid from (Maestro):

Card Security Number:                    Expires:

Signature:

Name  Mr/Mrs/Ms ...............................................
Address .............................................................
.........................................................................
.........................................................................
...................................... Postcode ...................

Daytime Tel No .................................................
Email ...............................................................

Valid to 31/12/12

**Can you help us with information about any of the Frith photographs in this book?**

We are gradually compiling an historical record for each of the photographs in the Frith archive. It is always fascinating to find out the names of the people shown in the pictures, as well as insights into the shops, buildings and other features depicted.

If you recognize anyone in the photographs in this book, or if you have information not already included in the author's caption, do let us know. We would love to hear from you, and will try to publish it in future books or articles.

**An Invitation from The Francis Frith Collection to Share Your Memories**

The 'Share Your Memories' feature of our website allows members of the public to add personal memories relating to the places featured in our photographs, or comment on others already added. Seeing a place from your past can rekindle forgotten or long held memories. Why not visit the website, find photographs of places you know well and add YOUR story for others to read and enjoy? We would love to hear from you!

**www.francisfrith.com/memories**

**Our production team**

Frith books are produced by a small dedicated team at offices in the converted Grade II listed 18th-century barn at Teffont near Salisbury, illustrated above. Most have worked with the Frith Collection for many years. All have in common one quality: they have a passion for the Frith Collection.

**Frith Books and Gifts**

We have a wide range of books and gifts available on our website utilising our photographic archive, many of which can be individually personalised.

**www.francisfrith.com**

# stretch PLAN

**For everyday health, fitness & sport**

THIS IS A CARLTON BOOK

Copyright © Carlton Books Limited 1996

10 9 8 7 6 5 4 3 2 1

First published in 1996 by Carlton Books Limited.

A CIP catalogue record for this book is available from the British Library.

ISBN paperback 1-85868-180-4
ISBN hardback 1-85868-160-X

**Executive Editor:** Lorraine Dickey
**Art Direction:** Zoë Maggs
**Photography:** Susanna Price
**Project Editor:** Ann Kay
**Production:** Sarah Schuman

Printed and bound in Italy

The publishers would like to thank the following companies for their generosity in lending sports equipment for this book: Olympus Sport, Reebok, Snow & Rock, Denver Athletic, and Surrey Cricket Centre.

# stretch
# PLAN

## For everyday health, fitness & sport

**CHRISSIE GALLAGHER-MUNDY**

CARLTON

# CONTENTS

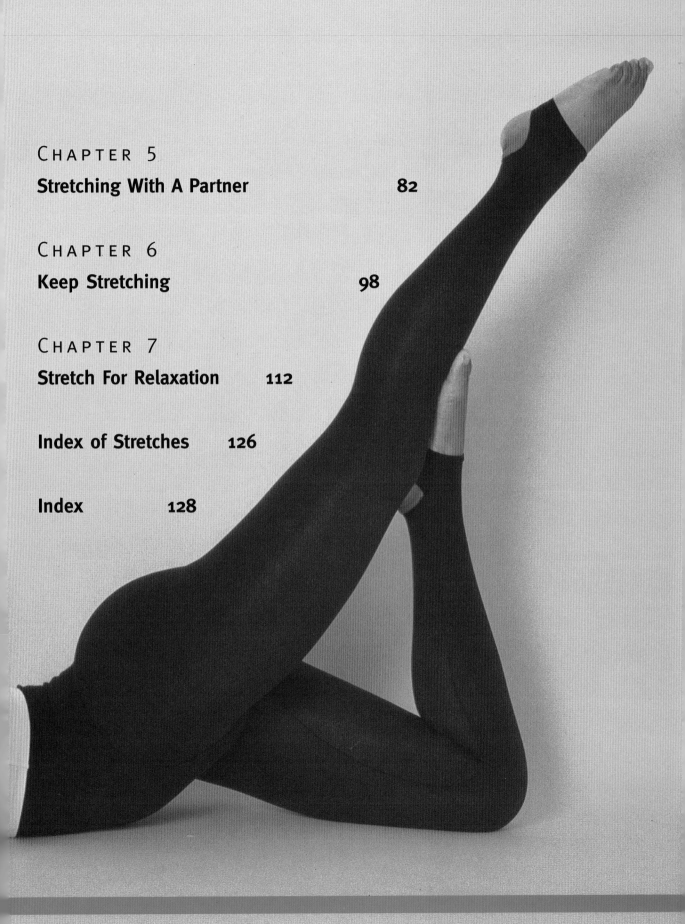

# introduction

What I hope everyone will do with this book is flick through it to grasp a general idea of the contents, read through it to increase their understanding of the subject – and then use it!

This book is informative; there are easily understandable descriptions of all kinds of stretching methods and specially choreographed photographs to inspire the reader. Above all, this is a practical manual which can help toward greater flexibility.

## PRACTICE MAKES 'FLEXIBLE'

Stretching, like all physical pursuits, requires practice. If you don't make the moves then you won't reap the benefits – so don't be tempted to just read this book like a novel and then put it down. You've got to get up and start putting it to the test! Try out the different methods suggested in this book to see which ones work for you and appreciate how good it feels to be moving and stretching those limbs!

You can start this book as a beginner or an experienced athlete – and whether stretching is a new concept to you or not, you will be enthused and informed by the explanations of stretch and the ways in which it can fit in as part of your daily routine and enhance different areas of your life. Did you know, for instance, that stretch can influence your posture and body image as much as it can improve your sporting chances?

In the first chapter you will find a definition of stretch and explanations that will clear up some of the misconceptions about stretching. This chapter will also give you plenty of reasons to improve your flexibility, both physiologically and mentally! Warm-up and mobility work is also covered, as these are essential parts of any good stretch programme.

## TRY AND TEST EVERYTHING

This book also provides you with a variety of methods for stretching. Some will increase your maximum flexibility and some will simply make you feel good. Either way there are chapters devoted to different stretching methods such as the PNF method, relaxation stretching and stretching with a partner – try them all and see which suits you best.

This book also provides you with a means of testing yourself and assessing your own flexibility level. Chapters 2 & 3 will help you to find your own level, your own shortcomings and help you set your own goals. With this information you can then use the beginners, intermediate or advanced level programmes, which allow you to mix and match and progress to the next level as your flexibility increases. Don't forget to practise regularly though...

## WARM UP AND COOL DOWN

If you are interested in any sport at all you will find some useful information in Chapter 4, which provides a comprehensive guide to the kind of stretches you should be doing prior to and after any major sporting activity. These stretches are specifically designed with specific sports in mind and will help to loosen the right muscles and enhance your sporting abilities. Many sports are covered, from Rugby to Skiing and Cycling to Golf. There are also some key stretches and mobilisers which should form part of all your pre- and post-sport stretch routines. Use this chapter often so that you memorise your stretches and can use them anytime, anywhere...

This book should be an inspiration to have some fun with your body! Take delight in feeling your body become more flexible and ready to move. Look at Chapter 5 for some ideas on how to work with a partner, or Chapter 6 for ways of getting yourself back to regular fitness and some unusual stretch ideas! There are stretches for problem areas and for relaxation purposes in Chapter 7. You can see already how many different ways stretch can be used.

## ON THE MOVE

At the very end of the book you will find some moving stretch routines which are designed to be done to the music of your choice and as a means of self-expression or relaxation. Learn these and you will begin to learn by heart all the other stretches in the book – you will never be short of ideas to move and keep supple.

I wish you fun and flexibility, but remember – keep this book accessible and ready for action. Don't leave it on your bookshelf – get down on the floor and use it!

Chrissie Gallagher-Mundy

# CHAPTER 1

# introducing
# STRETCH

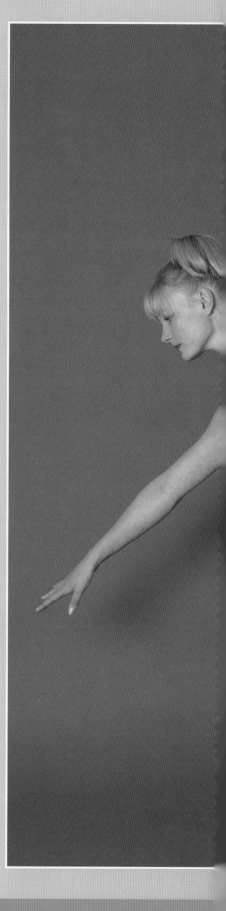

**The wonderful thing about stretching is that it can be so many different things to so many different people. It can provide a great starting point for getting your body into shape, an excellent all-round fitness programme, or the perfect complement to all kinds of sports and exercise regimes. However you choose to use it, you will no doubt discover that this is one of the most enjoyable forms of movement and exercise – and the perfect way to energize both the body and the mind.**

## A SENSE OF STYLE

Stretch forms a basic element of every major type of physical activity. This is especially true of activities where a certain physical "style" is important, where the shapes, movements, rhythms and dynamics that it is possible to express with the human body really come into their own.

The reason for this is that, unlike other elements of fitness, such as endurance-, stamina- or strength-building, stretch will begin to help you become physically and mentally aware of the shapes that you can create with your body. Stretch

does this by giving you an instinctive feel for the way in which your body is aligned – how various parts, especially the shoulder girdle, ribcage, pelvis and limbs, should naturally be placed.

## HAPPY MEMORIES

Once you understand a little more about stretching, you will find that it reminds you of whole areas of your body that you may have completely forgotten about over the years. For example, you will rediscover certain muscles that, once properly toned, can be used to lift and elongate the spine. This will help ease a whole range of posture-based problems, such as a painful back and aching joints. Stretching will also remind you of what it feels like to use your body as a tool, just as dancers do, allowing it to carry out the instructions that your mind is giving it, easily and without stress.

## A CO-ORDINATED APPROACH

Stretch also challenges your powers of co-ordination and simply shows you how good it feels to move freely. You will soon be enjoying the forms and lines that you can create with your body simply for their own sake – time at last to stop worrying about the precise shape of your figure or how many press-ups you can do! Now you can begin to take pleasure in the sheer joy of dance and movement.

You will find that stretch works on three main levels:

- to exercise every fibre of your muscles
- to exercise the tendons that join the muscles to your skeleton as well as the ligaments that connect one bone with another
- to tone your mind.

This is what makes it the perfect way to reawaken your whole system. If you have not exercised for a while, then this provides one of the very best ways to start a regular exercise programme. With its relaxing, meditative qualities it will provide you with so much more than many more competitive forms of exercise can... and it will keep you motivated for a long time to come.

## FIRST PRINCIPLES

Who should stretch? The answer is simple – everyone. Throughout this book, you will find programmes suited to people of all ages and abilities. It is, however, always a good idea to seek medical advice if you have any doubts at all about your fitness, or have any specific problems or injuries.

In this first chapter you will discover just what increased flexibility can do for you, in all kinds of different ways. You will also learn the all-important distinction between warming up and getting yourself moving fully – essential knowledge for anyone wanting a strong, supple body, free from injuries, aches and pains.

# what is
# stretch?

**WHAT'S THE DIFFERENCE?**

So, toning is all about contracting and overloading muscles, while stretching, by contrast, is all about extending and not overloading them. This doesn't mean that you simply opt for one or the other – stretch

Before going any further, the whole idea of stretch needs to be defined properly, especially as there are various common misconceptions about the subject. Stretching normally means elongating the muscles of the body. The muscles, tendons, ligaments and joint capsules of the body all stretch to varying degrees and this in turn can give an impression of the whole body feeling elongated, extended and lifted.

## TONING VERSUS STRETCHING

It is important to realize that stretching is not the same thing as toning. Toning the muscles involves contracting them – usually against some kind of resistance – in order to extend or bend a limb.

This process challenges muscles, and with practice they will respond by developing greater tone – that is, becoming stronger and more shapely. Remember that, if you want to increase muscle strength, there has to be a degree of "overload" – working the muscle until it tires and fails, so that it responds by growing stronger. For example, most people have well-toned biceps, at the front of the arm, because they are constantly working these muscles against resistance by picking up heavy objects.

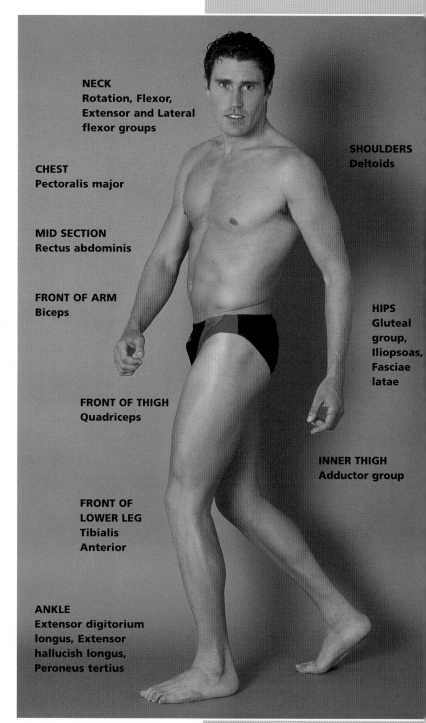

NECK
Rotation, Flexor, Extensor and Lateral flexor groups

SHOULDERS
Deltoids

CHEST
Pectoralis major

MID SECTION
Rectus abdominis

FRONT OF ARM
Biceps

HIPS
Gluteal group, Iliopsoas, Fasciae latae

FRONT OF THIGH
Quadriceps

INNER THIGH
Adductor group

FRONT OF LOWER LEG
Tibialis Anterior

ANKLE
Extensor digitorium longus, Extensor hallucish longus, Peroneus tertius

should always form a vital part of any toning programme. Anyone who has experienced weight lifting will know that maintaining the ability to stretch and reach should be developed alongside building strength. If this is neglected, the muscles tend to tighten up as they become larger and stronger, which will restrict the body's natural movement. This happens because, as a muscle contracts, it also shortens and in this tight state can be much more prone to stresses and injuries. The stretch element of a work-out programme should ideally return muscles to their pre-exercise length and state, making sure that they build up strong and long, rather than just bulky.

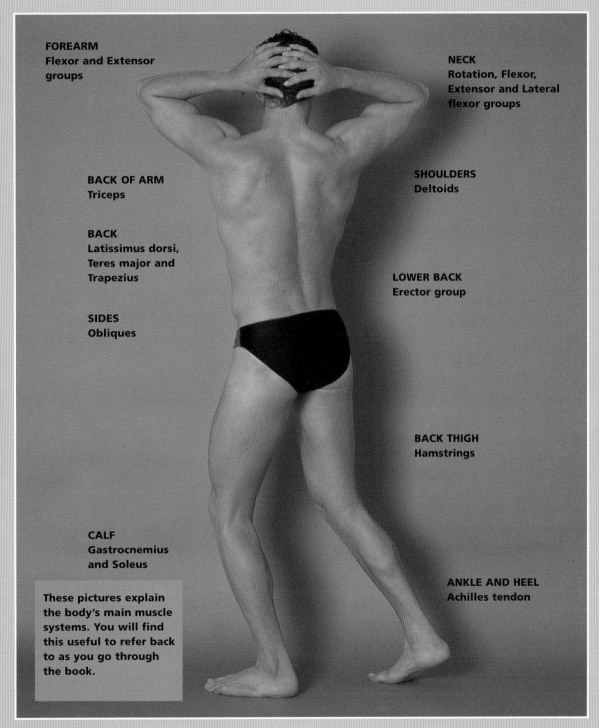

**FOREARM**
Flexor and Extensor groups

**NECK**
Rotation, Flexor, Extensor and Lateral flexor groups

**BACK OF ARM**
Triceps

**SHOULDERS**
Deltoids

**BACK**
Latissimus dorsi, Teres major and Trapezius

**SIDES**
Obliques

**LOWER BACK**
Erector group

**BACK THIGH**
Hamstrings

**CALF**
Gastrocnemius and Soleus

**ANKLE AND HEEL**
Achilles tendon

These pictures explain the body's main muscle systems. You will find this useful to refer back to as you go through the book.

# body and soul

There are also types of fitness programme aimed specifically at developing endurance and stamina. These usually involve some form of aerobic exercise, which is designed to increase the body's uptake of oxygen. Aerobic programmes place extra demands on the muscles – especially the major muscles of the limbs, the heart and lungs – as the body learns to utilize the oxygen more efficiently. If prolonged, this type of exercise also draws energy from the body's fat reserves. Running, climbing and swimming are all good examples of popular endurance activities.

## A STRONG BACK-UP

Stretching has no main part to play as part of an endurance activity, but it should always be used to provide a strong back-up. When muscles are worked hard they need looking after and soothing. Stretch sessions can give your muscles a vital rest-and-recovery period, helping to de-stress and relax them. And because stretching makes your muscles more pliant and flexible, there is much less risk of any injury or pain.

## TAKING UP THE CHALLENGE

Although you can begin to see how stretching is a crucial component of various different types of health regimes, don't lose sight of the fact that it is a challenge in its own right – and a challenge that can transform different areas of your life. Improving your flexibility so that all your movements become much easier should not only be an intrinsic part of any sport or work-out programme, but should also become a part of your everyday life.

## ANCIENT WISDOM

The benefits of stretch, for both the body and the mind, have been appreciated for thousands of years, and it is this double reward that make it so special. Many ancient forms of meditation and exercise, such as Yoga and certain Martial Arts, rely heavily on the body's ability to push the boundaries of suppleness back even further while maintaining both control and strength. There is no shortage of good physical and psychological reasons for you to take up stretch – and once you start, you are sure to think of a few more!

## A HEALTHY BODY

Physically, stretch will:

• **Return your muscles to their pre-exercised state and length**
• **Allow you a full range of movement, without restrictions**
• **Maintain this range of movement and so guard against aches and pains in the years to come**
• **Provide a warm-up for further exercise**
• **Provide a calm wind-down**

Psychologically, stretch will:

• Make you feel aware of your real self by putting you in touch with all of your body
• Lead you to discover the "whole" you by revealing the vital links between mind and body
• Put you at ease with your body by improving your range of motion and co-ordination. As you move and look better, so your sense of well-being will flourish
• Provide a form of exercise and relaxation that is non-competitive and easy to do, meaning that motivation should seldom be a problem
• Refresh your mind just as it energizes your body
• Provide an oasis amid life's stresses and strains, helping you to deal with them more effectively
• Ease your mind and body out of the various postures and positions that are causing all that mental and physical stiffness
• Feed your creativity – create shapes as you stretch and imagine yourself dancing, boxing, riding a horse; develop your fantasy life!
• Provide a pleasure that can be for you alone

session at the end of a work-out
• Keep muscles and joints mobile and flexible, and so reduce the risk of injury during exercise
• Improve your posture and physical alignment
• Improve the ease and quality of your movement
• Help to ensure a healthy back – many physiotherapists prescribe it!

• Help you to relax and unwind, relieving muscle tension
• Awaken muscles you never knew you had
• Provide you with a way of exercising that you can do almost anywhere and anytime, with friends or alone!

# towards total
# flexibility

Stretching is all about extending the body and its muscular framework; discovering your level and seeing if you can improve it. Have a go at some of the following simple exercises:

• Next time you are reaching upwards, downwards or across, try gently stretching just that little bit further – it's always possible if you make the effort.

• Make yourself aware of movements that you find hard to perform quickly without feeling a strain. For example, sit in a chair and try reaching down towards the ground as if a pencil has rolled under your legs. How does it feel? Or try standing at the foot of some stairs, with your hands firmly on the bannister, and place one foot on the first or second step. Now use your upper foot to lever yourself up. How high you go to start with obviously depends on the depth of the steps, but you should feel some stretch in your leg muscles. If you have no problems, try placing your upper foot on a higher step. Go gently and slowly, and don't do more than you feel absolutely comfortable with.

## YOUR PERSONAL STRETCH PLAN

These kinds of exercises will give you some indication of just how elastic your muscles are, and help to pinpoint restrictions that you might want to improve. Our bodies are excellent at making adjustments, and if you keep repeating certain movements over and over again, your muscles will start to respond and will learn to stretch further and further.

The best approach is to follow a personally planned pattern of exercises, aimed at stretching specific muscle groups. Use the Stretch Challenge in Chapter 2 to help you identify the areas that need work and to plan a programme of exercises and goals that is tailored to your level of ability and needs.

## STAYING MOBILE

To gain true flexibility, you need to use a combination of stretching and mobilizing. Mobilizing the body is not exactly the same as pure stretching, although it is closely allied. The emphasis is on movement in the joints rather than mostly in the muscles, and examples of good mobility would include:
• twisting around to see a passenger in the back seat of your car without feeling any twinges
• circling your arm past your ear painlessly and easily
• turning your head from side to side without feeling any "clicking" or pain.

Exercises aimed at improving mobility adopt a slightly different approach to stretching ones. They tend to consist of active movements, performed smoothly and consistently, whereas a stretch exercise involves assuming a position and holding it for a while to let the muscle elongate.

Mobility work will help to ensure that the synovial fluid that acts as a natural lubricant between joints is moving smoothly over the cartilage-covered, bony surfaces.

## MOVING WITH EASE

Once the body gets used to moving comfortably in a certain direction, the easier that movement becomes.

What happens all too often in everyday life is that we tend to get stuck in a rut of moving in very set patterns, repeating only a small range of movements that do not challenge all of our muscles. This means that certain muscles waste away, losing their strength and elasticity, and the mind-to-muscle co-ordination starts to slip. So, when we try to perform an action out of the ordinary – ouch! Suddenly there are twinges and stiffness where there shouldn't be any.

Keeping the body moving in all the directions it can is vital. Your body is rather like a metal puppet, which needs to be kept well oiled in order to maintain smooth and unhindered movement that can be carried out just when, where and how you want it. With a carefully balanced programme of stretch and mobility exercises, this is just what you can achieve.

# warming up

The kinds of mobilizing movements just described are best used as part of a warm-up routine. Warming up the body before any prolonged exercise is one of the most important elements to concentrate on if you want to move without injury. Take your warm-up at a calm pace, using gently rhythmic turning and rotating movements to get the body used to moving. You should be moving the joints slowly through their natural ranges of movement, as the cartilage surfaces become accustomed to moving over each other smoothly.

You may notice a few "clicks" and "pops" at the start of your warm-up (sometimes due to trapped gases between surfaces). As you continue, the synovial fluid works to lubricate the joint surfaces and you will find that the creaks and clicks start to disappear and the movement becomes much smoother.

## GETTING WARMER

The warm-up tells the rest of the body to get ready to move, and as everything gets into gear, you will gradually build up body heat. This increase in body temperature helps the muscles to become more pliable and supple, increasing the mechanical efficiency of your working muscles so that the contractions are more rapid and forceful. In other words, you are getting in touch with all those areas of your body that you may want to work effortlessly for you later on, so this warm-up puts you in touch – and in control!

## INCREASED BODY HEAT

**A warm-up improves the state of the body in preparation for further exertion. It does this by increasing the heat in the body's circulatory systems – which in turn improves blood flow and makes biochemical, nerve and muscular processes more efficient. It also helps along the metabolic process of fats and sugars.**

## THE JOINTS OF THE BODY

Our bodies have many different types of joint, with varying ranges of movement. Some are fibrous – bone connected to bone by fibrous tissue – while cartilaginous joints are connected by cartilage. Many of these joints only allow slight movement, or none at all. The joints that allow the greatest freedom of movement are known as synovial joints. In these, the end of each bone entering the joint is protected by cartilage and the joint cavity is lined with a synovial membrane. This membrane secretes a nutrient-rich natural lubricant called synovial fluid.

**The main synovial joint types are:**

**1. BALL & SOCKET**
Allows movement in all directions
e.g. Hip and shoulder

**2. HINGE**
Movement of a flex-and-extend nature only, e.g. Elbow

**3. PIVOT**
Rotation only, e.g. Head

**4. SADDLE**
All movement except rotation
e.g. Thumb

**5. ELLIPSOID**
Reduced ball & socket movement; virtually no rotation
e.g. Knee and wrist

**6. GLIDING**
Two surfaces gliding across each other
e.g. Joints between the vertebrae that make up the spine

# 2
CHAPTER

# finding your
# LEVEL

In this chapter you will find:

• a brief description of the various methods of stretching. There are different approaches available and some will suit you better than others. Some methods are also more appropriate at different times of the day or even at different stages in your life. There are more detailed explanations in the following chapters which will help you to understand a little more about the complexities of stretching and give you a chance to try the different methods safely.

• there is also a posture check which will teach you the correct starting position for all your stretch work. It will also help improve your general shape and stance and show you how to keep "lifted"

• a comprehensive flexibility test – the Stretch Challenge. This has been specifically designed to help you find

---

**FIRST THINGS FIRST**

Always go into moves slowly and cautiously, so that you and your body learn that stretch is a disciplined thing, and not something beyond your control or painful in any way. When you first begin, you may find even the mildest reach uncomfortable, but don't despair – it will simply be that your body is not used to the sensation of stretching. After a few sessions, you will soon find yourself getting used to the sensation, learning about your body and its limitations, and will feel more comfortable taking the stretch just that little bit further.

---

your personal stretch level and to help you identify areas of your body where you may find that you are stiffer than others. Once you are more aware of your strengths and weaknesses you can use this as part of your tools for putting together a programme that works on the exact areas you need as an individual.

# getting used to the stretch

## 1. THE BASIC STRETCH

The main aim of stretching is to lengthen and extend the muscles a little further than they would naturally extend by themselves. Either before or after physical exertion, it is always a good idea to lengthen the muscles and to feel the body reach and twist, so that you rid yourself of any tightness that may have built up in the joints.

Stretching should feel pleasant, not painful. The best general approach for a basic stretch is as follows:

• Find a comfortable stretch position that you can get into easily and hold without losing your balance. Try sitting with your legs apart and stretched out in front of you and then reach forwards, between your legs. This seated position is particularly good for beginners because your body weight is well supported and you will not be de-stabilized as you start to lean forwards. Also, the way your body weight is distributed tends to help the actual stretch.

• As you get into this stretch, you will feel some resistance in certain muscles (see the Stretch Reflex, p 22). When you feel this, just stay exactly as you are and simply register the tightness. Do not push yourself any further or come out of position. You should be feeling mild tension – just enough to tell your

brain that certain muscles are beginning to feel that they are being worked. You should not feel any pain. If you do, then return to an upright position and try again.

• After holding the stretch for 10-15 seconds, come out of it and return to your original sitting position. Now rest for 30 seconds, while gently moving the part of the body that you have just stretched – for example, in a seated stretch with legs astride, release the inner thigh muscles by slowly moving the legs in and out.

## 2. DEVELOPMENTAL STRETCH

This really means what it says: developing and holding the stretch a little longer so that the muscles lengthen even further. Follow these steps for the best results:

• Once again, take a comfortable seated position and start to lean in to your stretch until you feel mild tension and resistance.

• Hold the position until your body becomes accustomed to it – and keep breathing normally all the time.

• After 15-20 seconds, the tension should start to lift slightly and you will probably feel that you can lean a little further over. Don't push yourself; simply let your body weight ease you further over as you feel the muscle begin to lose some of its resistance.

The developmental stretch is really just a way of letting your body get used to the stretching sensation so that you can progress a little more, extending your stretch potential without discomfort or fear of injury. There are also various other ways that you can help your body to accept the stretch and extend it. For example, you will probably find it helpful to think about something other than the stretch while you are in position – a muscle will often complete its extension more easily if the brain is distracted briefly and the muscle just allowed to "release" naturally.

### NOW TRY THIS...

**Try this developmental hamstring stretch, which can be approached in two different ways:**

**1. BREATHE IT IN**
• **Lie on your back and hug one knee into your chest, really feeling the stretch in the groin area as you do so.**
• **Grasp your ankle and straighten your leg out as much as you can. Hold this position briefly, feeling the tension at the back of the leg, but only pull as far as you are able to without causing discomfort.**
• **Now breathe in slowly and, as you breathe out, pull the leg slightly closer to your face. It doesn't have to move a long way – just a few millimetres will do.**
• **Hold the position and repeat**

the breathing, pulling the leg closer still. Repeat this 3 times and you will be surprised at how much closer your leg is!

## 2. ROTATE AND STRETCH

Repeat as above, but instead of breathing in and out before you pull the leg in, get hold of the leg and simply rotate your foot first one way, and then the other. Now pull the leg further towards you. Repeat 3 times and notice how much further you are stretching your leg each time.

What both of these techniques illustrate is how the body and brain needs a little time to let the muscle achieve greater stretch. Also, this kind of stretching has a cumulative effect. If you repeat either of the above hamstring routines every day for just one week, and then do no exercise for two days (to allow the muscles to recover) and try the routines again, you will find that your hamstring muscles will feel much looser than ever before. And you can keep this feeling going – if you stick to a regular stretch programme.

# TAKING IT FURTHER

Here are some of the other principal ways in which you can develop your stretching abilities:

## BALLISTIC STRETCHING

This involves small bouncing movements that push the body further into its stretch. It is often looked on as highly controversial, because injury is more of a threat with this approach. However, ballistic stretching can be effective if carried out carefully, especially as a preparation for activities such as dance and martial arts – the gentle, pushing movements of the body aid further stretchiness and help prepare the body for more explosive actions. See pages 80-81 for more details on this method.

## PNF STRETCHING

This stands for Proprioceptive Neuromuscular Facilitation and is really just another way of "fooling" those muscles into relaxing a little more! If you contract a muscle strongly against a force for 10-20 seconds, its tone drops briefly immediately afterwards. If a stretch is applied at this point, you will achieve particularly good results. For more detailed directions see page 85.

## PARTNER STRETCHING

Stretching in company is an enjoyable way to pursue your stretch goals. You can work with anyone who is a similar size to you, even if your flexibility levels are different. What you must ensure is that you are both concentrating and working seriously to help each other.

The idea of working with a partner is to allow that person to use his or her strength to guide you into a deeper stretch – gently. If someone applies their extra body weight to yours, this can help to ease you into a more comfortable position, and sustained pressure will help the muscles to stretch further. There must, however, be lots of verbal and tactile communication between you so that everything is clearly understood and you stay within agreed limits. Specific routines and advice can be found on pages 82-97.

## RELAXATION STRETCHING

Stretching for relaxation may seem like a contradiction in terms, but the two actually compliment each other. Gentle stretching of stiff or tired muscles can be very relaxing to both the mind and the body – just the thing to revitalize and refresh you after a hard day's work! Although stretching and mobilizing are active pursuits, there are ways of assuming certain stretches that allow you to rest in those positions, letting your mind wander as your body really starts to relax.

Rather than being designed to develop flexibility, relaxation stretches are more to do with becoming at ease with the movement you already have. For full details of the many different stretches that you can relax into, and for other ways to relax a tired body, turn to Chapter 7.

# developing your stretch

One of the first steps towards developing your stretch technique is to improve your breathing, which will:

- calm you down
- help you maintain your stretches
- increase your stretching potential.

When you adopt a stretch position, don't hold your breath. Keep breathing normally and regularly, and check that you are doing this if you feel any muscular tightness. Holding your breath could increase your blood pressure, and it will certainly increase tension and discomfort and hinder the stretch.

## BREATHE DEEPLY

**To take a comfortable stretch position further, concentrate on breathing in slowly and deeply through the nose and then releasing the breath slowly through the mouth. Breathing acts as a good distraction technique when a stretch needs to be prolonged, making you concentrate on your breathing rather than on how your muscles feel. As you come out of the position, keep your breathing regular to prevent you from snapping out of a pose and possibly causing an injury.**

## DEVELOPING YOUR FLEXIBILITY

We all start out with pretty good flexibility – it's only through misuse or lack of use of certain areas of the body that we stiffen up. Once you are following your programme regularly, you should find stretching a pleasurable, relaxing thing to do and will start to become aware of your limits.

To increase your flexibility, you may want to include some developmental stretching – where you stay in a position a little longer to allow a specific muscle to stretch that little bit further. As before, always start with a warm-up, and bear in mind how some of the body's basic reflexes work.

## THE STRETCH REFLEX

When a muscle is stretched, it soon starts to send messages to the brain to tighten that muscle and halt the stretch, especially if it was sudden. This reaction is known as the stretch reflex. It is activated by a muscle's change in length and by the speed of the movement and is necessary not only to protect the body against over-stretching, but also to maintain muscular control during normal postures such as standing or sitting.

## AUTOGENIC INHIBITION

There is, however, another reflex that acts in opposition to the stretch reflex and this is known as autogenic inhibition. As the tension in stretching muscles increases, this is registered by special organs found in

the body's tendons (which attach the muscles to the skeleton). These organs send signals to the brain, telling the muscles to relax and preventing the stretch reflex from occurring. This reaction also stops muscles from contracting so hard that they pull away from the bone.

## PUTTING IT ALL TOGETHER

These two reflexes do not occur at the same time and everyday movement is unlikely to trigger autogenic inhibition. Both reflexes, however, do have an effect on how we should

stretch. Rapid or jerky stretches simply activate the stretch reflex and tighten the muscles, whereas smooth, sustained (30 seconds or longer) stretching of warm muscles allows them to relax and the stretch reflex to become desensitized. In the case of developmental stretching, autogenic relaxation will occur, overriding the stretch reflex.

The best way to perform a stretch is in a stable, comfortable position where some part of your body weight can assist you. For example, if the hamstring muscle of your right leg (see pp 10-11) is already quite

supple, but you wanted to develop it further, a good position might be to sit with your legs open and straight out to each side and your body leaning over your right leg. You can then perform the stretch slowly and gently, holding this position for 10-20 seconds. You might then be able to hold it for 30 seconds or more, letting the weight of your upper torso take you further as the muscles become less resistant. This kind of stretching really starts to develop your flexibility as it allows the muscles to relax gradually – and perfectly safely.

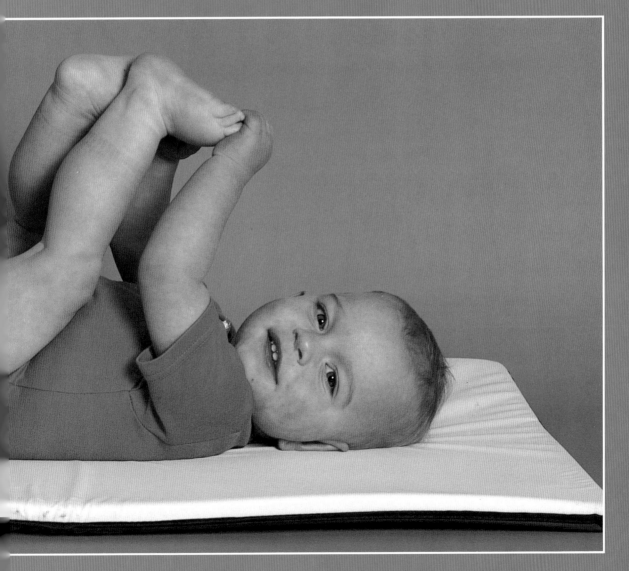

# perfecting your posture

Toning and lengthening your muscles not only leaves you feeling refreshed and revitalized but is also very important for good posture.

• In all areas of the body, it is important that muscles are pliable and flexible to avoid aches and pains – particularly if there are inflexibilities on one side of the body rather than the other. A stretching programme can really help to even up irregularities in the body – and also keep your stance correct and relaxed.

• To support the body in its natural alignment, you need stomach and back muscles that are strong but also flexible – not tight and bunched up. If the lower back muscles are very tight, and particularly if the stomach muscles are also weak, then the arch of the lower back may become too exaggerated. This in turn tends to make the ribcage bow outwards, throwing the body weight back over the heels so that the bulk of the upper torso's weight rests on the lower back. This can cause all sorts of back problems, as well as ugly posture.

## UNEVEN STRESSES

Similarly, if the buttock or hamstrings are very tight, the lumbar curve can be pulled too straight, causing uneven stresses and problems in the back and legs. Try lifting one leg off the ground, while keeping it fairly straight. Is this easy or can you feel tension and a pull on the pelvis, making it tuck underneath you? This feeling can be extremely restrictive and de-stabilizing. (If you do feel a tightness here, turn to the stretch index on pages 126-127.)

## PULL YOURSELF TOGETHER

Whenever you are sitting or standing in one place for any length of time, try to remember to pull up through the torso and the spine. Make sure your head is not arched back or collapsed forwards and that your stomach muscles are working and supporting the spine so that there is no pressure on the lower back.

Next, check for any major tensions that you might be feeling. The most common places for tension are the lower back, the back of the pelvis and across the shoulders. As well as noting the tension and seeking to release it by visualizing its release (see opposite page), this will also give you an idea of the areas you may want to stretch out later. For instance, if you have been hunched over a desk for a long time, it is always a good idea to take the body in the opposite direction – that is, arch backwards to relieve and extend the muscles.

## GENTLE BACK STRETCH

Try this relaxing back stretch.

• Lie on your back with your arms stretched out to the side, your legs bent and your feet flat on the floor.

• Now slowly lower your knees all the way over to one side and rest there.

• In this gentle twist position, you will feel the lower back release and the stomach muscles relax. You can now concentrate on slowly feeling all the muscles in your arms relax so that your shoulders sink towards the floor.

• There should be no stress in the neck or shoulders. One knee is resting on the other, so the legs are free of tension and the lower back is "opened up" slightly. If you were to rock the knees from side to side, resting for 10 seconds on each side, this would mobilize the back while providing a very relaxing and pleasurable exercise.

## REDRESSING THE BALANCE

To attain good postural stance, follow this routine.

● Stand with your back to a wall, with your heels touching that wall.

● Pull in on the stomach muscles and tilt the hip bones up toward you to help push your lower back closer to the wall. Check that the ribcage is pulled up, and has not sunk on to the hips. The shoulders should be relaxed, not held up or forced back. Drop the chin slightly to ensure that the top of the spine is straightened.

● Now take one step away from the wall and try to relax your body slightly. Stand there for a little longer and then start to embark on a mental journey through your body. Think first about your shoulders and about the muscles across the back of your neck and your upper back (see also pages 10–11). Picture the muscles lengthening and widening, even though you are not actually making any physical adjustments. Simply imagine the tensions being released in this area and the muscles expanding.

● Now picture a line running from the very tip of your head right down to the soles of your feet. As you stand there, this line is lengthening your spine – lifting the top of your head nearer to the ceiling while pressing your heels firmly into the floor. Don't make any physical adjustments, simply allow the illusion to release tensions and let the muscles learn how to extend and relax.

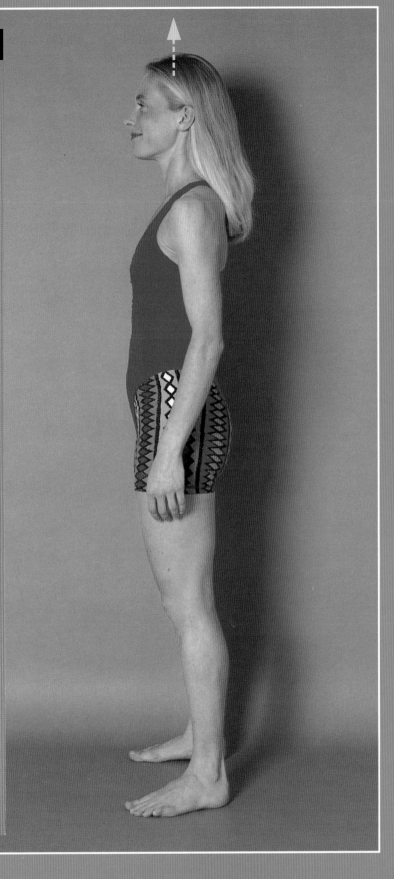

# the stretch
# challenge

Before you try to assess your flexibility, you should give yourself a little warm-up. We all stretch better when our bodies are warm and you want to know what you are really capable of, so give yourself the best possible chance!

● March up and down on the spot for 3-4 minutes and then continue to march but reach your arms first upwards and then downwards at the same time.

● Bend your knees and squat down, with your thighs no lower than parallel to the floor, and then reach up as high as you can. Repeat several times.

● Swing your arms across your body so that you twist first one way and then the other, making sure that only your upper body twists.

● Finally, go into a light, on-the-spot jog for 3 minutes until you feel your body warm up nicely, and the blood really flow inside you! While jogging, make sure that, as your foot hits the ground, contact goes from the toes to the ball of the foot and through to the heel. This helps to absorb any shock more effectively.

The four exercises featured on pages 28-31 are designed to let you assess your stretch capabilities so that you can then go on to devise a personal stretch programme in Chapter 3.

Once you are feeling properly warmed up, you are ready to take the stretch test.

Start with Exercise One (page 28), which is relatively simple, and work your way through to Exercise Four, on page 31. For each exercise, start out by attempting the Beginner's stretch, which has been colour-coded with a red background. Look at the photograph and try to get into a stretch that is as close to this as possible. Do not force anything and if you feel any part of your body threatening to cramp, come out of the position and "shake yourself out" before re-attempting it. When you are in the position, you should be able to feel a stretch, but no pain. You should also be able to hold this position for at least a few seconds while breathing normally and without feeling too much strain.

Between each stretch, you might want to shake yourself out and "jig" around gently before attempting the next position.

If you feel fully comfortable with the Beginner's position, then you might like to attempt the Intermediate position, always shown with a yellow background. Perhaps you find this quite easy, in which case move on to the Advanced position, with its blue background. Remember – don't push yourself.

As you go along, you should be keeping score for each exercise. Once you have found a position that reaches your limits, give yourself marks as to how comfortable and manageable that position really feels. For example, if you are happy with the Beginner's position and don't feel that you want to push this particular exercise any further, then mark yourself between 1 and 3, depending on how comfortable the position is. If you are happier at the Intermediate level, then give yourself a mark between 4 and 7, and so on, as shown below. What you should end up with is one score for each exercise.

| HOW TO SCORE | |
|---|---|
| BEGINNER: | 1-3 |
| INTERMEDIATE: | 4-7 |
| ADVANCED: | 8-10 |

## COMBINATION STRETCHING

Bear in mind when you try these four exercises that they are all combination stretches. This means that they do not focus on stretching one muscle, but can involve many muscle groups in different parts of the body. Since this is what is involved in most everyday and sports moves, then combination stretches are the best way to test yourself.

You may find that one part of the stretch is easier than another – this is because you are perhaps more flexible in one area than another. For the purposes of this test however, judge the stretch as a whole when you are deciding how comfortable and manageable it is.

Now look at the boxes on the right to further personalize your programme. Answer the questions in the boxes and this will help you to alter your programme so that in areas where you have slightly more flexibility (or less) you can take things a little further.

### EXERCISE ONE: WHAT YOU MIGHT FEEL

- **BEGINNER'S POSITION:** a stretch in the groin area.

- **INTERMEDIATE POSITION:** this requires some flexibility in the torso.

- **ADVANCED POSITION:** this also needs flexibility in the torso, and it also increases the groin stretch.

## EXERCISE ONE

**BEGINNER'S POSITION**

**INTERMEDIATE POSITION**

**ADVANCED POSITION**

# EXERCISE TWO

**BEGINNER'S POSITION**

**INTERMEDIATE POSITION**

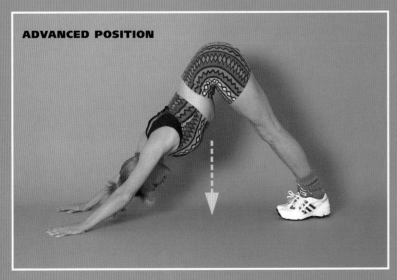

**ADVANCED POSITION**

## EXERCISE TWO: WHAT YOU MIGHT FEEL

- **BEGINNER'S POSITION:** a stretch up the back of the legs and in the shoulder area.

- **INTERMEDIATE POSITION:** you might feel an additional pull up the back of the calves.

- **ADVANCED POSITION:** you should feel extra tension in the back of the legs and some flexibility in the back.

# EXERCISE THREE

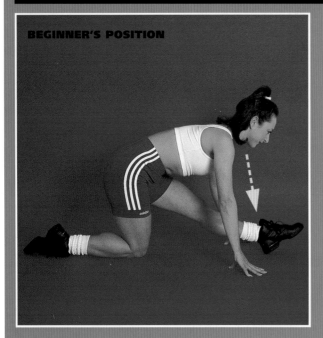

**BEGINNER'S POSITION**

**INTERMEDIATE POSITION**

**ADVANCED POSITION**

## ASSESSING THE TEST RESULTS

Once you have completed all four exercises, give your body a gentle, all-over shake and then march up and down on the spot, lightly, to release the muscles from their sustained positions. After any stretch session, including this one, make sure that you keep warm and rehydrate – so replace any clothes you have discarded and drink a large

### EXERCISE THREE: WHAT YOU MIGHT FEEL

● **BEGINNER'S AND INTERMEDIATE POSITIONS:** a stretch at the back of the legs and, depending on your flexibility, a stretch in the lower back area.

● **ADVANCED POSITION:** the same as above, plus additional flexibility in the groin.

**BEGINNER'S POSITION**

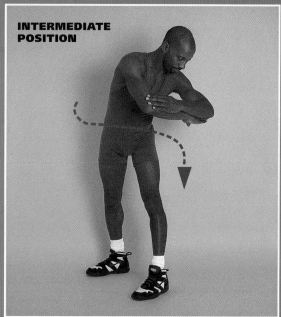

**INTERMEDIATE POSITION**

glass of water before you sit down and look at your scores.

You should now have a score for each of the four exercises. Add these scores together to give yourself one overall total and turn to pages 32-33 to discover which level of programme this score qualifies you for and how

you can tailor it to your own personal needs. Then turn to Chapter 3 to follow your programme to a stretchier you! Keep a note of what you scored on each individual test, as this will be used to add to your basic programme. When you have your programme, it doesn't matter what

level you start at – you will undoubtedly improve! Once you familiarize yourself with the exercises for your level and practise them regularly, you will probably find that you can reach the next level very quickly. To judge what progress you have made, simply redo the stretch challenge.

**ADVANCED POSITION**

### EXERCISE FOUR: WHAT YOU MIGHT FEEL

• **BEGINNER'S POSITION:** a stretch around the torso and back.

• **INTERMEDIATE AND ADVANCED POSITIONS:** an additional stretch in the back of the legs and hips.

# setting your level

Having worked through the exercises on the last four pages, you will now have an overall score. This score tells you which basic level you belong to.

## YOUR SCORE...

**A total score of 4-12:**
**BEGINNER'S LEVEL**

**A total score of 13-30:**
**INTERMEDIATE LEVEL**

**A total score of 31-40:**
**ADVANCED LEVEL**

Now you have identified your level, turn to Chapter 3 and study the stretch programme for that level.

Now look at the boxes on the right to further personalise your programme. Answer the questions in the boxes and this will help you to alter your programme so that in areas where you have slightly more flexibility (or less) you can take things a little further. This will ensure that your body is being stretched as far as it can in all directions while keeping things safe as you progress. Don't forget to pursue your programme regularly so that you notice the improvements.

**If you found any of the BEGINNER positions very uncomfortable or difficult:**

- Stay with your BEGINNER'S programme and work through it regularly. As you keep working, you will develop more stretchiness and if you go back to the Stretch Challenge exercises some weeks later, you may find that all the positions have become a lot easier.

**If you managed INTERMEDIATE level comfortably on Exercise 1:**

- Add Position 4 of the INTERMEDIATE programme in Chapter 3 to your schedule.

**If you managed ADVANCED level comfortably on Exercise 1:**

- Add Position 4 of the ADVANCED programme in Chapter 3 to your schedule.

**If you managed INTERMEDIATE level comfortably in Exercise 2:**

- Add Position 1 of the INTERMEDIATE programme in Chapter 3 to your schedule.

**If you managed ADVANCED level comfortably in Exercise 2:**

- Add Position 4 of the ADVANCED programme in Chapter 3 to your schedule.

**If you managed INTERMEDIATE level comfortably in Exercise 3:**

- Add Positions 1A and B of the ADVANCED programme in Chapter 3 to your schedule.

**If you managed ADVANCED level comfortably in Exercise 3:**

- Add Position 2, 2A and 2B of the ADVANCED programme in Chapter 3 to your schedule.

**If you managed INTERMEDIATE level comfortably on Exercise 4:**

- Add Position 5 of the INTERMEDIATE programme in Chapter 3 to your schedule.

**If you managed ADVANCED level comfortably in Exercise 4:**

- Add Position 3 of the ADVANCED programme in Chapter 3 to your schedule.

## GETTING PERSONAL

To personalize your programme to an even greater degree, go back and look at your individual marks for each exercise. Use them to make the adjustments shown on the right to the programmes outlined in Chapter 3. These adjustments apply whether your basic level is Beginner, Intermediate or Advanced.

## KEEPING NOTES

Make a note of all the exercises you should be adding to your programme. What you have now is a truly personal and challenging schedule which, if you follow it regularly, will develop your stretching abilities to the full.

You may find from attempting the tests that you identify an area of your body, such as the lower back or hamstrings, which is particularly stiff. Once you have made this useful observation, turn to Chapter 6 (and the Index) for stretches that are relevant to your specific problem area.

## SAFETY CHECK

**If you feel excessive pain in any of the stretches you have just tried, a check-up with your local physiotherapist would be a good idea. The physiotherapist can double-check that there are no muscle or bone injuries, or other conditions, that may be affecting your ability to stretch.**

# 3 your personal stretch PROGRAMME

Now that you know which basic level is just right for you, here are the three stretch programmes: Beginner, Intermediate and Advanced. You should be following most of one of these programmes, perhaps with some exercises borrowed from the other two to personalize your stretch routine even further (see pages 32-33).

## BEFORE YOU START

There are two important things to think about before turning to your personal programme:

**1. Breathing** – getting this right will help you to develop a really good technique (see page 22).

**2. The "stretch reflex"** – this gives you a greater understanding of how your body is reacting to the stretches (see page 22).

## LISTEN TO YOUR BODY

As you stretch, concentrate on what you are feeling – listen to your body. You should feel an extending sensation in your limbs when you take up the positions, but you should not feel pain. If you move into a stretch too quickly, or push too far, you will activate the stretch reflex (see page 22), which is the body's way of automatically protecting itself from over-stretching by suddenly tightening the muscles in question. If you always feel comfortable when you are stretching, you won't push too far and so will avoid unnecessary injury.

## TWO ALTERNATIVES

When you begin your programme, start slowly. Ease into the stretch and concentrate on listening to what your body is feeling. When you have held the position for the stated time, or for as long as it feels comfortable, come out of the stretch as slowly as you went into it and give your body a little shake. Then, if you want to, repeat the stretch once more.

There are really two ways of developing your stretch technique:

**1. Ease into a position,** hold it for the appropriate amount of time, and then release it slowly.

**2. Ease into the stretch** and then move around gently, perhaps rocking slowly in and out of the stretch, in order to get yourself used to the general feel of stretching. You might find that this is a good way to become comfortable with a stretch that you have never attempted before. Under no circumstances should you bounce, as this can traumatize or pull the muscles.

You must decide which of these methods – probably a combination of the two – works best for you.

## STARTING OUT

If you are doing a standing stretch, make sure you begin in the correct posture:

FEET should be flat, with the weight towards your toes. Ankles should be in line with your feet; don't let them fall outwards so that the weight is on the outside of the feet.

KNEES should always stay in line with the ankles. Thigh muscles need to be contracted so that the knees are pulled up and are stable.

HIPS should face towards the front (unless they are involved in a specific movement) and shouldn't be allowed to twist and put pressure on the knees.

● Try to check these things as you move into position and once you have assumed the pose.

● Whether you start a stretch sitting or standing, always reach upwards first – and really feel the space between each vertebrae in the spine as you raise your arms. In this way you begin with as much lift through the body as possible.

● If the stretch involves some kind of upper body curve, remember that the abdominal muscles play a great role in supporting the torso. Make sure that your abdominals are pulled in and your ribcage is lifted to give support and so ensure that there is no undue pressure on your back.

# beginner's stretch routine

When beginning your stretch routine, remember to find a warm, private room and start with a gentle warm-up. Make sure that your clothing allows you to move freely and try playing some inspiring music! You may want to use the annotated photos on pages 10 and 11 to guide you around the different muscles.

## POSITION 1: STORK STRETCH

• You might need to hold onto the wall or some other immovable object to help you balance as you reach behind to grasp your foot.

• Position the bent knee in line with the straight knee and pull the foot gently towards the buttock.

• You should feel a stretch along the front of the leg – this exercise is principally stretching the quadriceps muscles in the front of the thigh.

• If you feel a pull in the knee-cap, you may need to release the stretch a little.

• To increase the stretch, pull in on the stomach muscles and tilt the hips up and in, towards you.

• To include a groin stretch, start to tip your body forwards so that the bent leg and upper torso become parallel with the floor.

• Hold this position for 20-30 seconds, and then shake out your bent leg.

• Repeat twice on each leg.

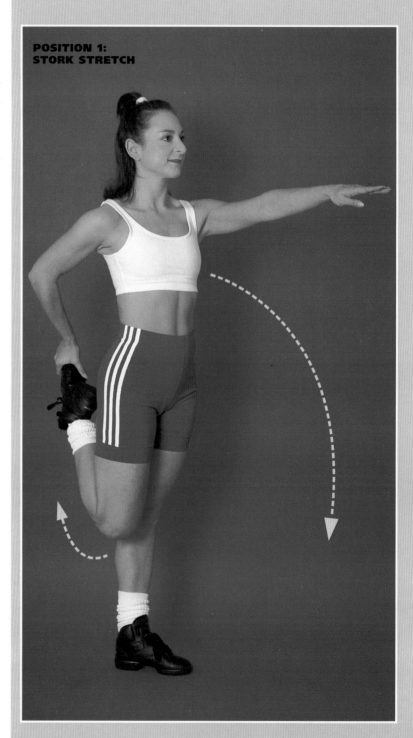

POSITION 1:
STORK STRETCH

## POSITION 2: CLOCK HANDS

- Keeping the raised leg as straight as possible, gently pull it towards your nose. If you can't keep your leg totally straight, don't worry, simply pull it in gently as far as you can without causing discomfort.
- You will feel a stretch at the back of the leg – this exercise principally stretches the hamstrings at the back of the thigh.
- Don't allow your hips to be pulled off the floor.
- To increase this stretch, breathe in slowly and, as you breathe out, pull the leg a little closer to you.
- Hold this stretch for 20-30 seconds and then relax the leg.
- Repeat twice on each leg.

## POSITION 3: WIDE STRETCH

- If you have trouble sitting with your legs apart while keeping your back straight, it may help to put your hands behind you to give you added support. Use the leverage of your hands to push your torso slightly forwards.
- If you have enough flexibility, place your hands on the floor in front of you; if this is too difficult, simply rotate your feet backwards as far as you can and release.
- You might feel this stretch in various places, depending on where you are tightest. You may feel some stretch in the lower back, the back of the legs or the inner thighs. This exercise principally stretches the adductors on the inner thighs.
- If you feel a harsh pull in the knee area, move your legs slightly closer together.
- Hold this position for 30 seconds.
- Repeat 3 times, but do a different exercise in between.

POSITION 2: CLOCK HANDS

POSITION 3: WIDE STRETCH

## POSITION 4: ARCHED STRIDE

- Make sure that you have the weight of your body pressed towards the front leg as you bend into your lunge, with your back toe acting as stabilizer. Now press your arms back behind your ears as far as you can.

- You will feel a stretch in the groin area as you hold your lunge, as well as a stretch in the shoulders. This exercise is stretching the adductor muscle group and the gracillis muscle on the inner thigh, and also the deltoids in the shoulders.

- Don't sink into the lunge but keep the body lifted and ready to push out of the stretch.

- Hold for 20 seconds before shaking out.

- Repeat 3 times.

## POSITION 5: BACK BEAUTY

- If you have not done this stretch before, stand in front of a wall and use this as a support by resting your arms against it. Keep your torso fully lifted as you arch slightly backwards. Pull up in your abdominal muscles.

- You will feel a flexing in your lower back and a stretch in the abdominals.

- You should not feel any pain – if you do, come out of it and try again without leaning so far.

- As you become more confident, you can start to arch slightly further, as long as your hips stay stable and you have a wall behind to stop you from falling too far.

- Hold for just 15 seconds.

- Repeat twice.

- Recover by lifting up and then curling your upper torso forwards.

POSITION 4:
ARCHED STRIDE

POSITION 5:
BACK BEAUTY

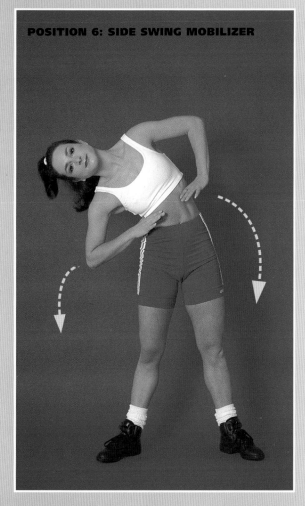

**POSITION 6: SIDE SWING MOBILIZER**

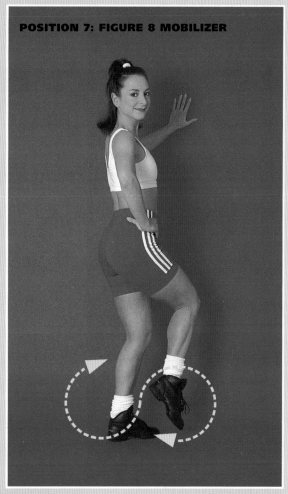

**POSITION 7: FIGURE 8 MOBILIZER**

## POSITION 6:
## SIDE SWING MOBILIZER

● This is a mobilizing exercise (see p 15) so, as you move gently from side to side in this position, you should be keeping a steady rhythm going.

● You should feel the sides of the body being stretched and the length of the torso becoming more flexible as you move.

● Don't bend so far that the sides of your body feel wrenched, and don't drop your head too far over – keep it in line with your body.

● Swing from side to side up to the count of 20.

## POSITION 7:
## FIGURE 8 MOBILIZER

● Holding on for support, swing your bent outside leg around in a large figure eight shape. First, your bent leg should swing forwards, across the front of your body, and then back in towards your other knee. It should then circle outwards, towards the back and around, so that your bent knee goes behind your straight leg, before coming back round to its starting position

once more. Let your supporting leg bend a little and keep your abdominal area lifted.

● The hip joint of your bent leg should be turning right round, and this is where you should feel the movement. It should also become easier and smoother as it continues.

● Keep swinging for 30-40 seconds, really reaching all parts of the figure 8.

● Repeat 3 times on each leg.

● This will help to keep the hip joints flexible and creak-free.

# intermediate programme

Start with a gentle warm-up. Once warm, keep lots of layers on and don't stop moving during your workout. Try using music to dictate some different tempos for the exercises that have more movement in them.

## POSITION 1: STEP UP

● Use a sturdy chair or stool to rest your foot on as you push your hips forwards.
● You will feel the stretch underneath the legs and groin, particularly the thigh of the leg on the floor – this stretch is for the adductors and hamstrings and the quadriceps.
● Hold the stretch for 15-20 seconds, shaking the legs out in between stretches.
● Repeat twice on each leg.

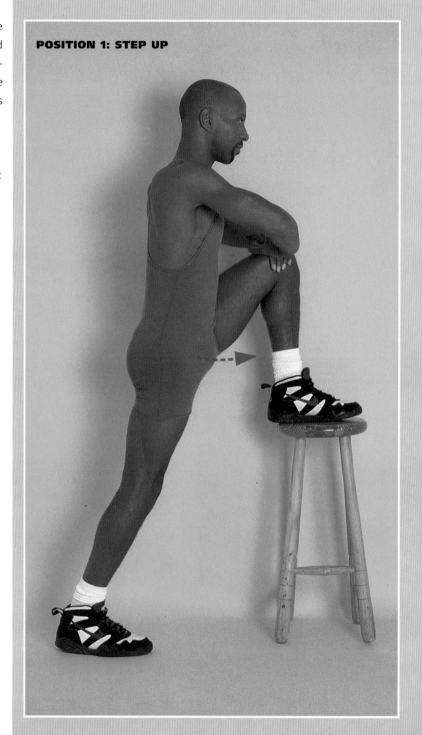

POSITION 1: STEP UP

## POSITION 2: FLAT OUT

- Start with your hands reaching high above your head and reach out as you start to bend over towards your leg. Try to keep your back as straight as possible as you lean over. When you can't go any further, rest your hands on your leg, above the knee.
- You will feel a stretch in the back of the raised leg and possibly also in the lower back. This stretch is principally to elongate the hamstrings at the back of the thigh.
- Don't round or collapse the back and let the head hang, but try to keep it as straight as possible, with help from the abdominal muscles.
- If you can rest your hands easily on your thigh, then you could gradually try to get near enough to rest your head there as well.
- Hold for 30 seconds.
- Repeat 3 times with each leg.

## POSITION 3: FORWARD CREEP

- With your legs outstretched and apart, see how far forwards you can lean and begin creeping further forwards with your hands to extend your stretch.
- You will feel the stretch on the inside of the legs – this stretch is for the adductors.
- You should not feel too much of a pull on the knees or the back of the legs – if you do, creep back slightly.
- If you let the weight of your torso pull you forwards and bow your head, the stretch will increase.
- Hold for 30 seconds and then come back and gently massage your inner thighs.
- Repeat twice.

POSITION 2: FLAT OUT

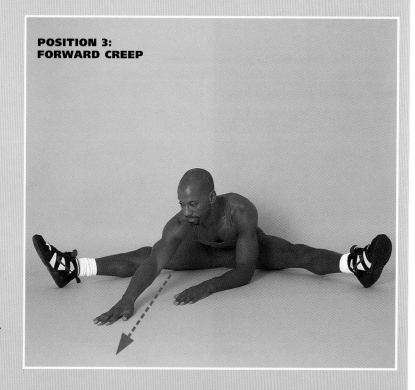

POSITION 3:
FORWARD CREEP

## POSITION 4: THE UPEND

• Link your hands behind you before you tip your upper body forwards and push your arms towards the floor.

• Keep your knees just slightly bent and you will feel a stretch on the back of the legs as well as the underarms. This stretch will extend the hamstrings and to a certain extent the deltoid, pectoral, biceps, Teres major and tricep muscle surrounding the humerus (the bone of the upper arm).

• Hold the position for a count of 16 and then bend the knees as you come upright.

• Repeat twice.

## POSITION 5: CURVACEOUS MOBILIZER

• Reach up as high as you can before leaning over to one side, but don't stop there – continue to curve the arm around to the front so that the upper body is curved forwards before it rolls to an upright position.

• You should feel a pleasurable stretch in the upper back and side of the torso – this movement will stretch the trapezius and rhomboid major, which are the main muscles in the upper back.

• You can let the stretch involve more of the back if you curve further over as you come round to the front. Make sure, however, that you keep the abdominal muscles pulled up and stable.

• Repeat 5 times each side.

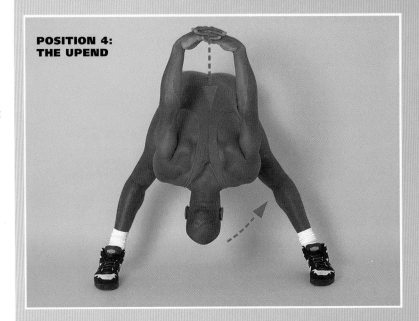

POSITION 4:
THE UPEND

POSITION 5:
CURVACEOUS MOBILIZER

## POSITION 6: THE SWING MOBILIZER

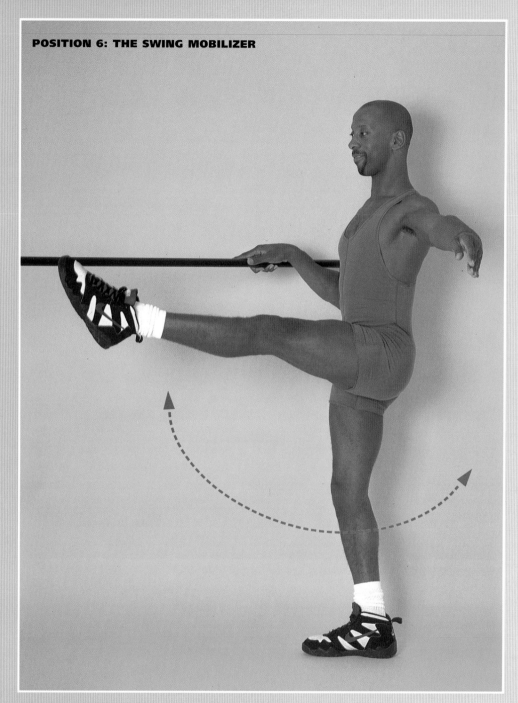

### POSITION 6:
### THE SWING MOBILIZER

• Always make sure that you are warmed up for this mobilizer.
• Stand tall, holding on to a bar, for support and gently swing your leg back and forth, at a low level.
• You will feel the leg loosening in the hip and the front and back of the thigh stretching slightly.
• Make sure that the swing is the same height at the back as it is to the front.
• Try to keep the knee of the supporting leg as straight as you can and keep the hips still – do not let the pelvis be pulled underneath.
• Do 8-10 swings on each leg.

# advanced programme

Make sure that your body is warmed up and comfortable before you start your programme. Move into the positions carefully and try to make the transition from one pose to another as smoothly as possible.

## POSITION 1: THE CRAB

- Step backwards into a lunge, with the back leg straight, and lower your hips as close to the ground as possible. Make sure your front knee is directly over your toe.
- Now swivel inwards a quarter of a turn so that your bent knee is out to the side of your body and your hands are reaching out in front.
- You will feel a stretch in the groin area and the inner thighs and some working of the mobility in the hips. This stretch combination mainly involves the adductor groups, the hamstrings, gluteals and quadriceps.
- Don't allow the bent knee to turn inwards once you are in the second pose and make sure the knee of the straight leg is facing the ceiling.
- If you want to increase the stretch, keep the heel of your bent leg flat on the floor.
- Move into the first position and hold for 15 seconds, then move into the second pose and hold for 10.
- Repeat by turning back into the first pose and repeating the sequence.

POSITION 1A: THE CRAB A

POSITION 1B: THE CRAB B

## POSITION 2A: WALKABOUT A

## POSITION 2: WALKABOUT

- Sit as far forward as you can in the first pose shown (2a), keeping both buttocks touching the floor.
- Keep the back as flat as you can as you extend the arms forwards on to the floor.
- You will feel a stretch in the lower back as well as in the hip joint of the bent knee, and possibly on the inner thigh of the straight leg.

## POSITION 2B: WALKABOUT B

**POSITION 2C: WALKABOUT C**

## POSITION 2: WALKABOUT CONTINUED

• Next, turn towards your extended leg and pull your chest towards your leg (2b). Breathe out as you press as far over as you can. Then gently release. Finally come back to the centre before extending your second leg. Now breathe in and as you breathe out press the chest and arms forwards pushing the chest as near to the floor as your inner thighs will allow (2c). From 2a-2c you will feel a stretch in the sides of the legs (the inner thighs and at times the outside of the thigh) and also in the sides of the torso and possibly the back. This will involve the adductor muscle groups, the hamstrings, the gluteals, the quadriceps, the oblique muscles of the abdomen and the Latissimus dorsi.

• You should feel a gentle pull in these areas – not pain.
• Hold each pose for 20-30 seconds and move smoothly into the next. To recover, use your hands to push you up and your abdominal muscles to help your back curl back up gently to an upright position.
• Repeat this sequence on each leg twice.

## POSITION 3:
## ROTATING MOBILIZER

- Pull up in the knees and keep the legs straight and the hips fixed as you rotate your upper torso around that axis. Start by rotating at a shallow angle and build up to a rotation position where the back is parallel with the floor at all times. This is a very advanced exercise, so it will take some practice.
- You will feel the upper torso mobilizing and every part of the torso being stretched. The exercise involves the oblique and rectus abdominal muscles and the Latissimus dorsi.
- Rotate once each way, return to an upright position, and breathe especially deeply.
- Repeat 3 times.

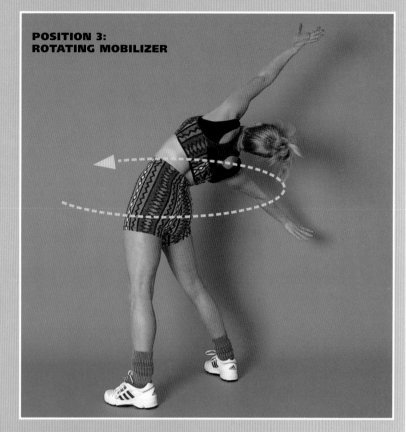

POSITION 3:
ROTATING MOBILIZER

POSITION 4: OLYMPIC STANCE

## POSITION 4:
## OLYMPIC STANCE

- Holding on for balance if necessary, reach behind and hold onto the calf. Now, keeping the leg behind you, start to lift and straighten it as far as you can.
- This requires great flexibility in both the front and back of the legs, the groin area and the lower back. It involves the hamstrings, gluteals, quadriceps and the adductor muscle group.
- Raise the leg only as high as you can without losing balance and tipping forwards too far.
- Stretch into the position slowly.
- Try the position twice on each leg.

# making stretch a habit

If you have never tried a regular stretch programme before, you need to develop good habits from the beginning.

• Set a regular time aside for your routine. Allow yourself a small amount of time to begin with – 15-20 minutes is plenty – so that you are less likely to postpone the work-out just because you haven't enough time.

• Find a comfortable place where you can avoid interruptions. Your chosen spot should be warm, draught-free and with enough space for you to stretch out in all directions.

## GETTING STARTED

When you are ready to start your programme, place the book in front of you and make sure you have warm clothing on that won't restrict you. Start with a quick warm-up, by following the example on page 26 or by doing whatever it takes for you to feel warm and loose. A jog is a good way to warm the body and its muscles, as is a quick spell in a sauna or steam room, if you have access to one.

Whenever you stretch, make sure that you are concentrating fully. Turn the answerphone on so that you don't have to leap up quickly if someone calls – one of the easiest ways to pull a muscle! Begin the stretch in a comfortable, stable position and stay warm. A mirror may be useful, to check that you are in the correct position, but is not absolutely necessary. And always make sure that you can get out of the position before you get into it.

## MOVING ON

As you continue with your stretching programme, your body will become more accustomed to the moves and you should find the stretches becoming smoother. You should also find yourself stretching farther, but always make sure that your hands (or other body parts) are there for support, so that there is no risk of slipping or lack of control.

Don't be too impatient for results and always stretch with caution. You should feel the stretch sensation in the belly of the muscle rather than at the extremes. If you feel too much of a pull at the joints, for instance the back of the knees, insides of elbows or deep in the lower back, then ease off slightly. With regular practice you will get to know your body and its warning signs – a correct stretch feels pleasurable rather than painful.

After your stretch session, you should feel thoroughly revitalized, relaxed and perhaps a little hungry. The next day, you should feel no ill effects. If you are stiff or have aches and pains, then you could well have overdone it. You do not want to damage or tear your muscle fibres – so start GENTLY.

## GETTING GOOD RESULTS

Stretching must be done regularly and correctly for it to make a real difference. If you do your stretch programme properly, there is no reason why you shouldn't practise a short session as frequently as every other day if you want to see some rapid results. A day's rest in between is always a good idea to let the muscles recover. The great thing is, elasticity in the muscles really can improve pretty quickly – you will be surprised at what you can achieve in as little as two weeks.

## MOVING TO MUSIC

Try using different pieces of music to match your mood. In this way you can make your routine a relaxing end-of-the-day stretch one day and a revitalizing pick-me-up the next!

# 4 sporting CHANCES

CHAPTER

**Whatever sport you enjoy, there are stretches you can do that will help you to get even more out of your sporting activities. What you will find here are stretches specially designed to enhance warm-up and cool-down procedures for your chosen sport. As you will see from flicking through this chapter, every sport has its own specific stretches, and most activities also have some stretches in common.**

Turn first to the core stretches and mobilizers on pages 53-57, and use these as part of your warm-up routine, to prepare yourself for exertion. Now turn to the stretches designed specifically for your sport and work your way through these. At the end of these, you should be prepared for anything the game or activity can throw at you!

## FLEXING YOUR SPORTING MUSCLES

Most sports utilize the large muscles of the body. These include the deltoids (shoulders) and the pectorals (the chest area) as well as the abdominals (the stomach area) and the major leg muscles: quadriceps, hamstrings and calf muscles;

gastrocnemius and soleus. (Refer to pages 10-11, for a guide to the major muscles).

## WARM UP AND COOL DOWN

As we have already mentioned, stretching is not a substitute for a proper warming up procedure – but it is an important part of the warming up and cooling down process. When you begin whichever warm-up routine you use before your chosen sport, you should start by doing the moves that are aimed specifically at increasing your body temperature.

You should now start with the core stretches and core mobilizers outlined on the following pages. These will continue the warm-up process and help your body and mind to rehearse the kinds of moves you will be making in your sporting activity. This is why the stretches shown in this book are as close to actual sports moves as possible. If you can keep your stretches similar to the actual moves you may be making, then your body will be that much more prepared.

## BEFORE...

Once you have performed your sports stretches, you are ready for your game, so, if you are not due to play immediately, wear something warm to keep the thermal effect going a little longer. If you get

delayed enough for the muscles to start cooling down, you may have to repeat a few more stretches just to get you moving again.

## ...AND AFTER

After your game, you will be hot and your muscles will be warm and "buzzing". This is not, however, always the best time to stretch out. Although your body is warm immediately after hard exercise, the muscles are tightened due to repeated contraction. Try to give yourself 10-15 minutes to re-adjust and cool down; just walk around slowly and let the muscles rest.

Once you feel rested, you can begin your cool-down stretches. Repeat some of the core stretches and mobilizers included in the section for each sport. Adopt the position and ease into it gently. You are aiming to gently extend the muscles to their pre-exercise length and rid them of any tension gained during exercise. While you are performing these stretches, you are giving yourself a mental and physical breathing space – perhaps to think about your game and the improvements you can make next time around.

Only stay in the stretch for as long as feels comfortable; feel the muscles release instead of trying to develop the stretch. After a hard game is not the time to go for a developmental stretch.

## A WORD OF WARNING

Sports coaches and sporting organizations are finally beginning to realize the benefits of a regular stretching routine. Even so, there are a lot of bad practices around – so don't always follow what you see on the T.V! As a first step, attend reputable stretch classes if you can; doing that, combined with using this book, should give you a good grounding in some basic do's and don'ts.

# coping with
# stiffness

Muscle stiffness can come in many forms: from the not so painful to the excruciating! It can range from the odd twinge in one muscle or another to an overall ache that might make you feel that you have a bad case of flu.

## THE DEBATE CONTINUES

There is still a great deal of debate over what exactly causes muscle stiffness. One theory is that it is caused by over-worked or over-stressed muscle fibres sustaining microscopic tears. While these tears gradually repair themselves, the healing process produces general soreness. Other theories talk about muscle "ascemia" – a build-up of bodily chemicals, such as lactic acid, that could send the muscles into spasm and cause stiffness.

What is known for certain is that, as with most things that occur in the body, the reaction sets in at a later stage. This means that, with severe stiffness, the pain may actually come on one or two days after the strain

## WHEN DOES STIFFNESS STRIKE

You may well experience stiffness if:

• you have played a particularly hard game
• made a move that your body wasn't used to
• not played your sport for a while.

has taken place and sometimes even increase during the third day. This is known as D.O.M.S. or Delayed Onset of Muscle Soreness.

## WHAT CAN YOU DO?

Theories on the best way to deal with stiffness also differ, although it is generally accepted that very stiff muscles need time to recuperate. So, if you have done a hard work-out, it is best to spend the following day letting the body relax and the muscles recover. If you do feel soreness, then muscle rubs, saunas or a hot bath can help relieve some of your aches. If the pain or stiffness is really troublesome, then Aspirin or Arnica (a natural healing agent) may help.

## THE HAIR OF THE DOG

If you really have to be active on a day when you are very stiff, then the best way to deal with the aches and pains is to warm up thoroughly and then go carefully but firmly into some of the moves and stretches that you did the day before. If you work through the same moves that made you stiff, it will help to relieve your stiffness so that you can exercise with less pain.

If you have an actual injury such as a muscle tear, then pursuing your sport on the same day is probably not advisable and rest may be more appropriate. If in any doubt, rest up – or see a doctor.

## AVOIDING STIFFNESS

Some tips on avoiding stiffness:

• It is thought that reducing the amount of "eccentric contractions" – extending the limb against resistance – in your work-out [for example, holding a 5 kilo dumbbell in bent arm position and extending the arm slowly twenty times] may well help to prevent severe stiffness.
• If you train regularly, the body seems better able to adapt and severe stiffness reduces considerably.
• An adequate cool-down and stretch-out period reduces the risk of severe muscle stiffness.
• Heat and massage can help relax and rejuvenate tired muscles, flushing fresh blood through to the stiff areas, which then carries away potentially toxic – and thus stiffness-inducing – products.
• A hot shower immediately after exercise reduces stiffness more effectively than waiting until you get home to have a shower.
• The main cause of stiffness is people throwing themselves into routines they are unprepared for and being over-enthusiastic on the first few sessions. Pace yourself, give your body time to adapt and save your enthusiasm for regular, sustained training, not short sharp bursts!

# core
# stretches

Use these basic stretches as part of your warm-up and cool-down routines, before and after your sporting session. These core stretches should be followed by the core mobilizers on pages 56-57 and then by the warming up and cooling down stretches designed specifically for your sport. You can also use the core positions as part of your warm-ups and cool-downs before and after any kind of fitness activity, such as a stretch session or aerobics workout.

**Whatever kind of stretch you are doing, it is important to remember that:**

• your posture should be good, with your body properly aligned – follow the photos carefully for this

• you are as relaxed as possible when you begin each move

• you should keep breathing normally throughout all your stretches.

## WATCH YOUR POSTURE

Many of the curling, bending or leaning movements may involve one part of the body without affecting others. However, there are plenty of movements that work several different areas, and bad posture in one will affect the others. In some of the more complicated stretches, you may be tempted to let your overall posture go as you try to increase your stretch, but you must always maintain the proper alignment of the

body in order to stretch the correct muscles and avoid the risk of injury. NB: "Work-out" refers to any form of exercise or sporting session.

## POSITION 1: THIGH STRETCH

• Extending your arm will help you balance in this position.

• You should feel a stretch sensa-tion in the front of the thigh.

• To increase this stretch, check that both knees are level, pull in on the stomach and tuck the hips up and under, towards you.

**Before Your Work-out:**

Hold for 20 seconds.

**After Your Work-out:**

Hold for 30 seconds.

POSITION 1:
THIGH STRETCH

## POSITION 2: BASIC LUNGE

• Once you have mastered this basic stretch, it will lead you into many other stretch combinations.

• You should feel a stretch in the groin area and in the back of your calf.

• The lower you go in this position, the more you will increase the stretch, but make sure you don't lose your balance.

**Before Your Work-out:**

Hold for 20 seconds.

**After Your Work-out:**

Hold this stretch for 25 seconds.

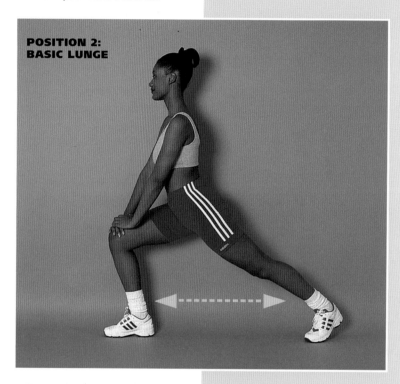

POSITION 2:
BASIC LUNGE

## CHECKING YOUR FACTS

Because many of the stretches featured in this chapter are combination stretches, stretching out several muscles or body areas, the exact muscles stretched are not listed. If you need to know the muscle names, check the area of the stretch and refer to pages 10-11, where the annotated photos will help you to identify the muscles used.

## BALANCING ACT

A lot of the sports stretches need a good sense of balance, so bear these points in mind.

• Balancing is not just a question of luck – you can develop the skill by using the muscles in the right way and it gets much easier with practice. It is especially important to use your abdominal muscles. Strong abdominals, used to keep the torso lifted and supported, is the key to good balance.

• Concentrate on "growing tall" and pulling up through the spine – drawing strength from the abdominals – whenever you want to balance on one leg. Or you can try this position as a separate exercise, to improve your overall sense of balance.

• In the last position, help yourself by focusing your eyes on one spot and pulling in on the stomach to give you a strong base from which you lift upwards.

• If you are standing on one foot, imagine that there is hardly any weight on that foot and that the top of your head is pressing upwards.

• Balance becomes much easier with practice.

**POSITION 3:
WIDE PLIÉ**

## POSITION 3: WIDE PLIÉ

• Press the knees well out over the toes and make sure the feet are completely flat – no rolling!

• You should feel a stretch across the whole groin area.

• The lower you go in this position, the more you will increase the stretch.

**Before Your Work-out:**

Hold for 25 seconds.

**After Your Work-out:**

Hold for 30 seconds.

## POSITION 4: SPINE STRETCH

**POSITION 4:
SPINE STRETCH**

• In this pose you are reaching up as high as you can, lifting the weight off the pelvis and ribcage and feeling the spaces between the vertebrae extend.

• Don't allow the back to arch too far, this is an upwards stretch.

• You should feel the spine length-ening, plus a stretch through the limbs – imagine that you are grow-ing taller.

**Before Your Work-out:**

Hold for 25 seconds.

**After Your Work-out:**

Hold for 20 seconds.

Now you have completed your basic stretches, move onto the mobilizers before you tackle your sports stretches.

# core
# mobilizers

## POSITION 1: KNEE CIRCLES

• Hold onto the knee caps and gently guide the knees in a clockwise direction and then back the other way. Bend the knees to help you.
• This will help warm up the knee and leg area.

**Before Your Work-out:**
Repeat 3-4 times in each direction.

### DO THE TWIST

In order to get the most out of any twist move, one part of the body must be fixed so that the other part of the body has something to twist from or against. Usually, this means fixing the knees and hips in a forward-facing position and allowing the upper torso to rotate above it.
In this way the knee and hip joints are protected by not being pulled out of line.

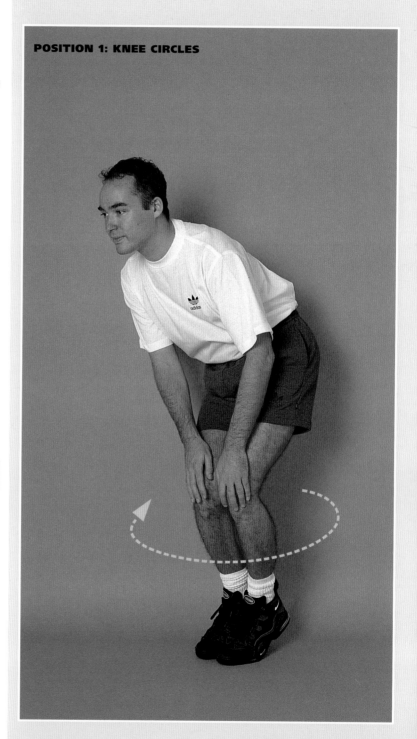

**POSITION 1: KNEE CIRCLES**

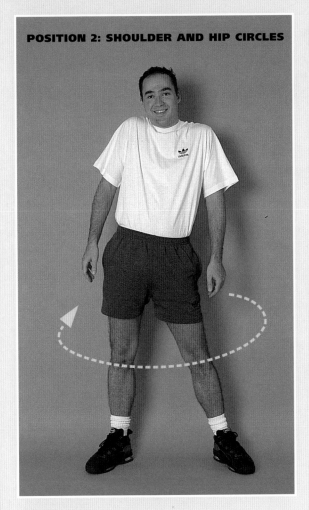

**POSITION 2: SHOULDER AND HIP CIRCLES**

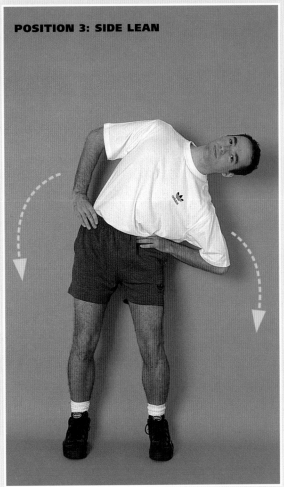

**POSITION 3: SIDE LEAN**

## POSITION 2:
### SHOULDER & HIP CIRCLES

• Move the shoulders in large circles: hunch them right up to the ears, press them back behind you, squeezing the shoulder blades together, and then push them down and forwards. As you are doing this, circle your hips at the same time, moving them backwards out to one side and then around to the front and out to the other side.

• This will mobilize and loosen the shoulder and hip areas.

**Before Your Work-out:**

Repeat 5-6 times in each direction. (Not needed as a cool-down.)

## POSITION 3: SIDE LEAN

• Tip the top half of the torso from side to side, gently taking it slightly further each time.

• Do not flop; gently feel the stretch up the sides of the torso.

**Before Your Work-out:**

Repeat 8-10 times.

**After Your Work-out:**

Repeat 4-5 times, more slowly.

Now that you have completed your basic programme you can turn to your sports stretches to finish your pre (and post) stretch routine.

# SPORTS stretches

Look through all the sports, as you may find that a particular stretch in a sport you don't do is just as applicable to you in your chosen activity.

## POSITION 1: STRETCH

Good for sliding tackles, high kicks and general flexibility on the field.

**BEFORE YOUR GAME:** Hold for 30 seconds.

**AFTER YOUR GAME:** Hold for 25 seconds.
• Stretches the groin area and back of thighs.

POSITION 1

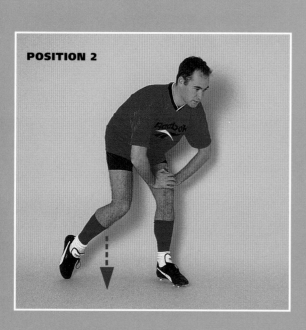

POSITION 2

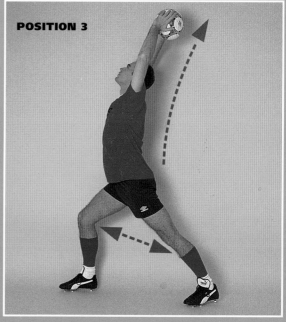

POSITION 3

## POSITION 2: STRETCH

Good for all running and kicking moves.

**BEFORE YOUR GAME:** Hold for 25 seconds.

**AFTER YOUR GAME:** Hold for 30 seconds.
• Stretches the front of the lower leg and ankle
• Keep the toes tucked underneath you as you press down on the back foot.

## POSITION 3: MOBILIZER

Good for throw-ins and general flexibility on the field. Step into and out of this position.

**BEFORE YOUR GAME:** Hold for 30 seconds.

**AFTER YOUR GAME:** Hold for 35 seconds.
• Stretches the groin area and legs, chest and arms.

POSITION 4

POSITION 5

## POSITION 4: MOBILIZER

Good for general flexibility to prevent injury, particularly to the hamstrings.

**BEFORE YOUR GAME:** Hold for 30 seconds.

**AFTER YOUR GAME:** Hold for 35 seconds.
• Stretches the lower back area and also backs of legs.

• Try rolling the ball slightly away from you to increase the stretch in the lower back and then roll it in between the feet to feel more of a stretch at the back of the legs.

## POSITION 5: STRETCH

Good for leg and back flexibility to prevent injury.

**BEFORE YOUR GAME:** Hold for 40 seconds.

**AFTER YOUR GAME:** Hold for 30 seconds.
• Stretches the backs of the legs and lower back. You may feel it in the calfs.

## POSITION 6: STRETCH

Good for stretching out the buttocks for kicking and fast running.

**BEFORE YOUR GAME:** Using one hand for balance, hold for 30 seconds  Repeat on each leg.

**AFTER YOUR GAME:** Try adopting this same position sitting down on a warm surface and hold for 35 seconds. Repeat on each leg.
• Stretches the buttocks and side of thighs.

POSITION 6

### A LITTLE RELIEF

When performing more extreme stretches, for any sport, a gentle rubbing or pummelling of the area stretched, after release, will help bring blood to the area and provide instant relief for any discomforts.

## POSITION 1: MOBILIZER

**Good for snaps and scrums**

**BEFORE YOUR GAME:** Hold for 30 seconds each way.

**AFTER YOUR GAME:** Hold for 20 seconds.
• Stretches the chest, torso and hips.

• If you alternate from side to side quite quickly, this move will also serve as a mobility exercise, mobilizing waist and hips.

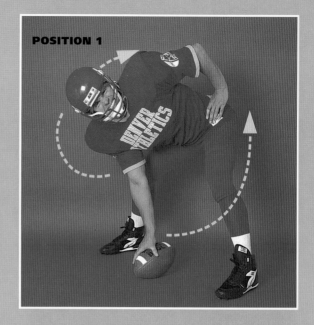

POSITION 1

## POSITION 2: STRETCH

This stretch is good for kicks, sprints and general game flexibility.

**BEFORE YOUR GAME:** Hold for 30 seconds each leg.

**AFTER YOUR GAME:** Hold for 35 seconds each leg.
• Stretches the backs of legs and groin.

• You can use the ball to help you or, if you want a greater stretch, then place the hands on the floor.

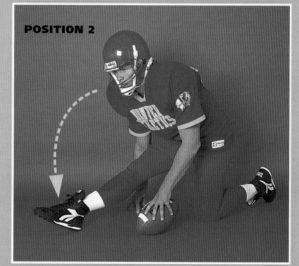

POSITION 2

## POSITION 3: STRETCH

Good for kicking, running and preventing injury to the ankle area.

Gently press one heel into the floor while pressing the ball of the foot into the floor and lifting the heel of the other foot.

**BEFORE YOUR GAME:** Perform alternating presses for 1 minute.

**AFTER YOUR GAME:** Slow the movement down and hold each foot down for 8 seconds each foot. Repeat 5 times.

• Mobilizes ankles and stretches the Achilles tendons.

POSITION 3

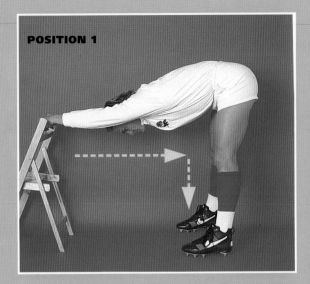

POSITION 1

## POSITION 1: STRETCH

**Good for kicking, scrums and sprints.**

**BEFORE YOUR GAME:** Hold for 40 seconds.

**AFTER YOUR GAME:** Hold for 35 seconds.
• Stretches the backs of the legs.

• Use the back of a chair or, if you're outdoors, use a tree or wall to let you bend forwards.

POSITION 2

## POSITION 2: STRETCH

**Good for general game flexibility as well as for kicks and falls!**

**BEFORE YOUR GAME:** Hold for 30 seconds
each leg.

**AFTER YOUR GAME:** Hold for 35 seconds each leg.
• Stretches the buttocks and the side of the leg.

• The more you pull the legs towards you, the more you will feel a stretch.

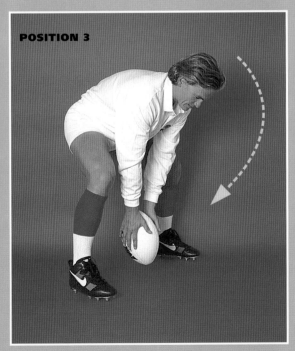

POSITION 3

## POSITION 3: MOBILIZER

**Good for all the bending involved in scrums.**

Swing the ball all the way up above the head and down between the legs, bending the knees.

**BEFORE YOUR GAME:** Swing the ball 15 times.

**AFTER YOUR GAME:** Swing the ball 10 times.
• Mobilizes the legs, hips and arms.

## POSITION 1: STRETCH

Good for back-hand and net shots.

**BEFORE YOUR GAME:** Hold for 30 seconds each arm.

**AFTER YOUR GAME:** Hold for 35 seconds each arm.
• Stretches the shoulder and upper back.

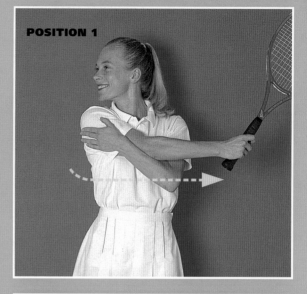

POSITION 1

## POSITION 2: STRETCH

Good for serves and overhead smashes.

**BEFORE YOUR GAME:** Hold for 15-20 seconds.

**AFTER YOUR GAME:** Hold for 15 seconds.
• Stretches and limbers the back and spine.

• Ease the racket slowly down the back to increase the stretch. Keep the hips still and the pelvis tucked under.

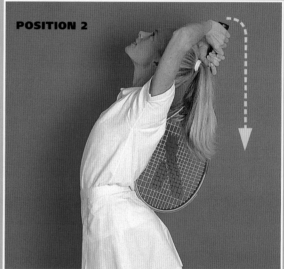

POSITION 2

## POSITION 3: MOBILIZER

Good for alternating back and forehand shots.

**BEFORE YOUR GAME:** Swing and hold for 15 seconds each side, twice.

**AFTER YOUR GAME:** Hold for 20-30 seconds each side.
• Stretches the sides and front of the torso

POSITION 3

**POSITION 4**

## POSITION 4: STRETCH

**Good for your service swing and overhead shots.**

**BEFORE YOUR GAME:** Hold for 20 seconds.

**AFTER YOUR GAME:** Hold for 20-30 seconds.
• Stretches the chest and arms and promotes shoulder mobility.

**POSITION 5**

## POSITION 5: MOBILIZER

**Good for achieving a good grip, a strong serve and general control of racket.**

Swing the racket over to one side, bringing it horizontal, and hold; then swing back the other way, bringing it again to a horizontal position and holding.

**BEFORE YOUR GAME:** Repeat 8 times.

**AFTER YOUR GAME:** Repeat 8 times.
• Mobilizes the wrists and helps prevent strain in this area.

**POSITION 6**

## POSITION 6: STRETCH

**Good for serve and overhead volley.**

Bring the racket forwards and then press it back into the position shown, pressing as far as your shoulders will allow.

**BEFORE YOUR GAME:** Repeat 10-12 times.

**AFTER YOUR GAME:** Hold for 15 seconds. Repeat twice.
• Stretches and mobilizes shoulders and promotes flexibility across the shoulder area.

**POSITION 1**

**POSITION 2**

## POSITION 1: STRETCH

**Good for teeing off, as well as flexibility and ease of movement on all golf strokes.**

**BEFORE YOUR GAME:** Twist one way and hold for 15 seconds.

**AFTER YOUR GAME:** Hold for 20 seconds on each side.
• Stretches and mobilizes the torso and waist.

• Keep the hips facing forwards and make sure the knees remain forwards and are not pulled out of line.

## POSITION 2: STRETCH

**Good for putting and pitching and driving from the tee.**

Use your golf club to allow your lower arm to pull the top arm further back and so increase the stretch.

**BEFORE YOUR GAME:** Hold and pull down with the bottom hand for 10 seconds, then swap arm positions.

**AFTER YOUR GAME:** Hold for 15 seconds each arm.
• Stretches the shoulders and back of arm.

• Don't allow your back to arch as you reach behind.
• Keep your legs wide to provide an inner thigh stretch at the same time.

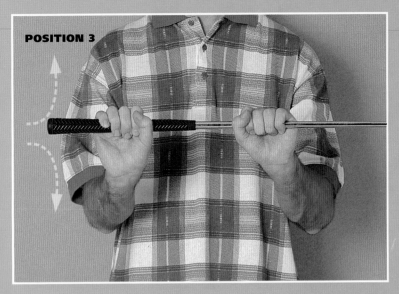

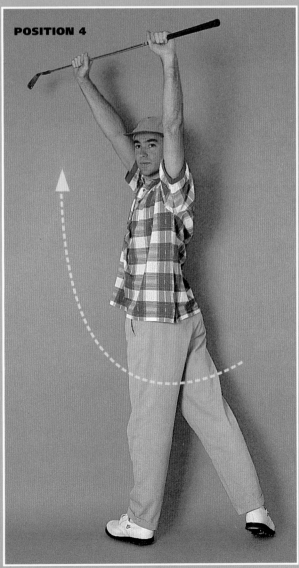

## POSITION 3: MOBILIZER

**Good for wrist flexibility, which is essential for control of putting and driving strokes.**

Hold the club equally in both hands and lift and lower the wrists as far as possible each way, while keeping the forearms still.

**BEFORE YOUR GAME:** Flex up and down 15 times.

**AFTER YOUR GAME:** Flex up and down 20 times.
• Mobilizes and strengthens the wrists and forearms.

## POSITION 4: MOBILIZER

**Good for all-round playing flexibility.**

Hold onto the club and give a real swing down and up to one side, letting the movement twist the body as it might in a real driving shot. Make sure, as you reach the top position (as in the photo), that you are fully stretched through your whole body and that there is a good twist in the waist.

**BEFORE YOUR GAME:** Swing to each side 8 times.

**AFTER YOUR GAME:** Swing to each side 8 times.
• Mobilizes the torso and legs.

ALL OF THESE STRETCHES APPLY TO BOTH SPORTS

## POSITION 1: STRETCH

**Start by going into the lunge position with back leg bent. Then reach the arm over towards your head to twist the torso slightly into a sideways leaning position.**

Good for exactly what you might expect from the position – bowling – in both sports.

**BEFORE YOUR GAME:** Hold for 20 seconds and repeat twice on each side.

**AFTER YOUR GAME:** Hold for 30 seconds on each side.
• Stretches the groin and the back, the Achilles and the side of the torso.

POSITION 1

## POSITION 2: STRETCH

**Good for general leg flexibility for cricket and for runners' slide techniques in baseball.**

**BEFORE YOUR GAME:** Hold for 30 seconds.

**AFTER YOUR GAME:** Hold for 40 seconds.
• Stretches the back of the straight leg and the outside thigh and buttock area of the bent leg.

• Use the bat to push yourself further down over the straight leg. When you have really developed your stretch, you can loop the bat over the foot to stretch even further!

POSITION 2

## POSITION 3: MOBILIZER

**Good for bowling, batting and throwing-arm mobility.**

Start with both arms raised above the head and bring one forward as you press the other backwards so that each inscribes a full circle, passing each other at the top.

**BEFORE YOUR GAME:** Continue movement for 40 seconds.

**AFTER YOUR GAME:** Continue movement for 30 seconds.

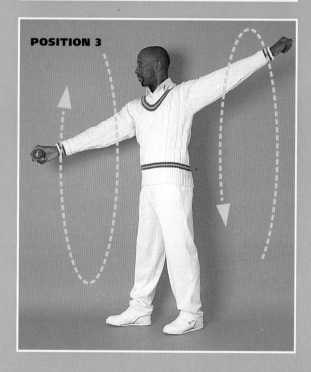

POSITION 3

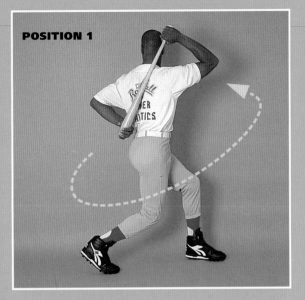

## POSITION 1: STRETCH

**Good for the wind-up bowl in Baseball, batting in cricket and all the twisting movements involved in both sports.**

**BEFORE YOUR GAME:** Hold for 20 seconds on each side.

**AFTER YOUR GAME:** Hold for 30 seconds on each side.
• Stretches shoulders and most of the upper torso; also mobilizes the legs and the hips.
• Pulling the bat up or down slightly will increase the stretch on either shoulder.

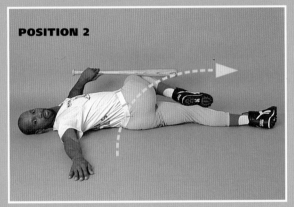

## POSITION 2: STRETCH

**Good for twisting movements, for example the swing and follow-through for throwing, batting etc.**

**BEFORE YOUR GAME:** Hold for 20 seconds on each side.

**AFTER YOUR GAME:** Hold for 40 seconds on each side.
• Stretches across the torso around to the lower back and also the buttock of the bent leg.
• If it is more convenient, you can do this position standing. Use the bat to pull that leg further across the body, while keeping the opposite shoulder pressing back into the floor.

## POSITION 3: MOBILIZER

**Good for bending, scooping and running.**

Bend into the squat position and then press the legs straight again, keeping your knees in line with your toes and without rolling on your feet.

**BEFORE YOUR GAME:** Perform 10 squats up and down.

**AFTER YOUR GAME:** Perform 3 squats very slowly up and down.
• Mobilizes legs and hips and develops overall flexibility.
• Use the bat to provide counterbalance, so that you can really get the squat position correctly – that is, weight well over the heels as you bend the knees (not lower than 90 degrees).

## POSITION 1: STRETCH

**Good for catches and overhead throws.**

**BEFORE YOUR GAME:** Hold for 15 seconds, repeat 5 times.

**AFTER YOUR GAME:** Hold for 20 seconds.
• Stretches the stomach and mobilizes the lower back.

• Use the weight of the ball to ease yourself gently backwards.

POSITION 1

## POSITION 2: STRETCH

**Good for sprinting and jumping.**

**BEFORE YOUR GAME:** Hold for 20 seconds on each leg.

**AFTER YOUR GAME:** Hold for 30 seconds each leg.
• Stretches the back of the thigh of the straight leg and the outside thigh of the bent leg. Also stretches across the upper back.

• Use the ball in this position to extend the stretch slightly further by rolling the ball away from you and then in again.

POSITION 2

## POSITION 3: MOBILIZER

**This is an advanced mobilizer. Perform this carefully, pulling up and in on the abdominals for support. Good for throwing, kicking and fast bending movements.**

Circle the ball all around the body in a complete circle. Bend as much to the sides and back as you do to the front.

**BEFORE YOUR GAME:** Circle one way 5 times and back the other way 5 times.

**AFTER YOUR GAME:** Circle more slowly, 3 times each way.
• Mobilizes waist, hips and most of the torso.

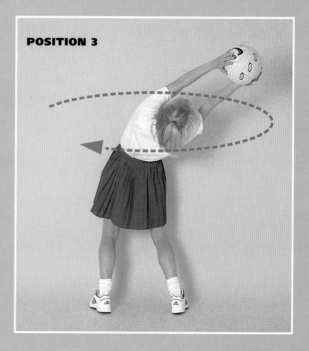

POSITION 3

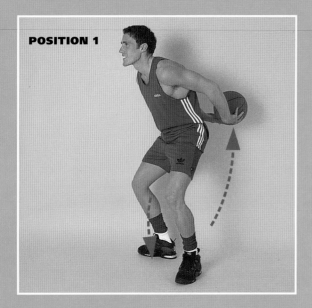

POSITION 1

## POSITION 1: STRETCH

**Good for arm flexibility and throwing moves.**

**BEFORE YOUR GAME:** Hold for 20 seconds and repeat twice.

**AFTER YOUR GAME:** Hold for 30 seconds and repeat twice.
• Stretches the chest and underarm/shoulder area and also warms the legs.

• Press the knees out over the toes as you lower into this plié position. Keep the hips in between the legs (as opposed to a squat, where the backside is behind the heels), then raise the ball as far behind you as you can, keeping the arms straight.

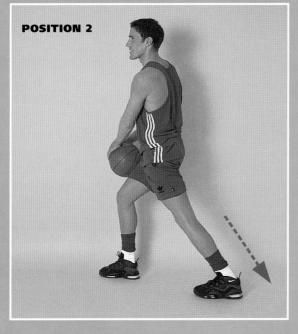

POSITION 2

## POSITION 2: STRETCH

**Good for running, jumping and gaining speed (in any sport).**

**BEFORE YOUR GAME:** Hold for 20 seconds and repeat on each leg.

**AFTER YOUR GAME:** Hold for 30 seconds and repeat on each leg.
• Stretches the calf and Achilles tendon in the ankle (which is one of the few ligaments you can stretch slightly).

• This may look like a short lunge position, but the emphasis here is on the calf and ankle of the back leg. So bend your front knee and then press the back foot down slowly so that you feel a stretch in the calf muscles.

POSITION 3

## POSITION 3: MOBILIZER

**Good for leaps, bends and dodges.**

Start by holding the ball up high above the head, stretching through the spine. Now swing the ball down with arms outstretched and swing it between the legs, following with your head.

**BEFORE YOUR GAME:** Swing down and up 15 times.

**AFTER YOUR GAME:** Swing down and up 10 times.
• Mobilizes the hips, legs, arms and shoulders.

POSITION 2

## POSITION 1: STRETCH

This is an advanced stretch. Good for sustained cycling, which uses a lot of leg power.

**BEFORE YOU CYCLE:** Hold for 10 seconds.

**AFTER YOU CYCLE:** Hold for 30 seconds
• Stretches the front of the thigh.

• If you're outside, use a wall or tree to do this stretch against.

## POSITION 2: STRETCH

Good for uphill riding and dismounts, and for when there is weight on the back wheel, which puts stress on the back, Achilles area and calf.

**BEFORE YOU CYCLE:** Hold for 20 seconds, on each leg and keep the arms in position to feel the stretch in the forearms.

**AFTER YOU CYCLE:** Hold for 30 seconds, on each leg.
• Stretches both the inside of the forearms and the Achilles and ankle.

• Note the position of the arms and the left leg and foot. This ensures that you are stretching two completely different areas at the same time.

POSITION 3

POSITION 4

## POSITION 3: STRETCH

Good for "log hops", "bunny hops " and wheel pivots, where the body is curved forward and the neck is pulling back on the shoulders. This stretch will help redress the balance.

**BEFORE YOU CYCLE:** Hold for 10 seconds.

**AFTER YOU CYCLE:** Hold for 30 seconds.
• Stretches and limbers the lower back in opposition to the position that you must sustain constantly when actually cycling.
• You can hold onto the cross bar or the saddle, whichever is most comfortable in this position, but above all ensure that you are stable.

POSITION 5

## POSITION 4: STRETCH

Good for dismounting while moving and rising across a camber.

The first half of this exercise consists of lifting the leg up onto the cross bar with the leg well-bent, then for the second part, keep hold of the bike, and press it away from you by straightening the bent leg.

**BEFORE YOU CYCLE:** Hold the first position for 10 seconds, and then the second one for 15 seconds.

**AFTER YOU CYCLE:** Hold the first position for 15 seconds and then the second one for 25 seconds.
• Stretches the groin area at first and then, as you straighten the leg, you will feel it at the back of the leg.

## POSITION 5: MOBILIZER

Good for keeping the hips and legs mobilized.

Swing the leg forwards and back, keeping the hip from lifting and making sure that the movement is smooth.

**BEFORE YOU CYCLE:** Swing the leg gently each way 15 times.

**AFTER YOU CYCLE:** Swing the leg gently each way 25 times.
• Mobilizes the hips and gently stretches the back and front of the legs.

**Note:** when riding downhill and doing rocks and drops, the shoulders are lower and the head is pulled back, so it is very important to stretch the neck. Pay particular attention to the neck stretch on page 110.

POSITION 1

POSITION 2

## POSITION 1: STRETCH

**Good for breast stroke and in-the-water flexibility.**

**BEFORE YOUR SWIM:** Hold for 20 seconds.

**AFTER YOUR SWIM:** Hold for 30 seconds.
• Stretches the front of the upper arms and chest, also the groin and inner thigh area.

## POSITION 2: STRETCH

**Good for all of your strokes.**

**BEFORE YOUR SWIM:** Hold for 20 seconds.

**AFTER YOUR SWIM:** Hold for 30 seconds.
• Stretches all across the upper back area.

• Hold your towel or clasp the hands to really make the most of this stretch.

## POSITION 3: STRETCH

**Good for freestyle stroke and general leg flexibility in the water.**

**BEFORE YOUR SWIM:** Hold for 30 seconds each side.

**AFTER YOUR SWIM:** Hold for 40 seconds each side.
• Stretches the back of the straight leg, the outside of the bent leg and the torso.

• Make sure you get the twist on the upper body as well as the lean over towards the straight leg.

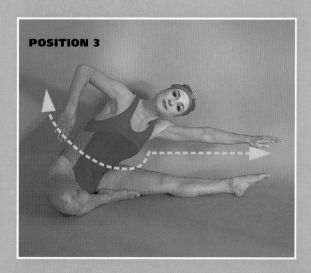

POSITION 3

POSITION 4

## POSITION 4: STRETCH

**Good for all strokes.**

Make sure that you are in a stable lunge position. If you now tilt the hips slightly towards the bent leg, you will feel a stretch along the inner thigh of the straight leg.

**BEFORE YOUR SWIM:** Hold for 20 seconds. Repeat with lunge on the other side.

**AFTER YOUR SWIM:** Hold for 30 seconds. Repeat on the other side.
• Stretches the area underneath the shoulders as well as the inner thigh and groin area.

• Lift the arms as high as you can behind you to stretch the shoulders and chest.

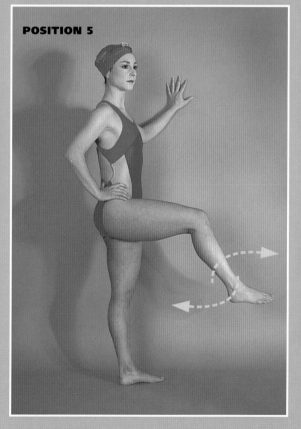

POSITION 5

## POSITION 5: STRETCH

**Good for strong leg kicking and leg work in the water.**

Standing in the water, simply flop your ankle backwards and forwards against the resistance.

**BEFORE YOUR SWIM:** Continue movement for 30 seconds on each leg.

**AFTER YOUR SWIM:** Continue movement for 40 seconds on each leg.
• The drag provided by the water will stretch the muscles around the ankle and gently massage the calf.

## POSITION 1: STRETCH

Good for all the leg-work required in skiing to keep you in a streamlined position. This needs strong thighs and this stretch will ensure that the large quadricep muscles are properly stretched out and so kept from becoming bulky or prone to cramp.

**BEFORE YOU SKI:** Hold for 25 seconds on each leg.

**FOR YOUR APRÈS-SKI:** Hold for 35 seconds on each leg.
• Stretches the front of the thigh and the ankle of the bent leg.

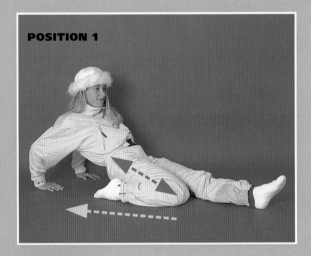

POSITION 1

POSITION 2

## POSITION 2: STRETCH

Good for ankle mobility and flexibility – ankles sustain a lot of pressure when skiing.

**BEFORE YOU SKI:** Hold, with control, for 25 seconds.

**FOR YOUR APRÈS-SKI:** Hold for 35 seconds, resting your hands against a steady wall instead.

• Stretches the ankle and calves.

• You can do this stretch either in and out of skis, but you will get further with skis on because they support the forward incline. Make sure the rest of your body is taut and don't allow the stomach area to bow outwards.

POSITION 3

## POSITION 3: STRETCH

**Good for transversing moves and slide-slipping.**

**BEFORE YOU SKI:** Hold for 15 seconds.

**FOR YOUR APRÈS-SKI:** Hold for 35 seconds without boots on, keeping the ankles straight.
• Stretches the sides of the torso and the side of the leg and ankle.

• In ski boots you can do anything! As you take a curving bend over to one side, let your boots lean slightly to give you some stretch up the side of the ankle and use your pole, digging into the snow, to balance you. (If you do topple over, your hip should hit the snow first!)

POSITION 4

## POSITION 4: STRETCH

**Good for stretching out the inner thighs after all those static knee parallels and work with the quadriceps. Also good for snowploughing turns.**

**BEFORE YOU SKI:** Hold for 15 seconds.

**FOR YOUR APRÈS-SKI:** Hold for 35 seconds without boots on, keeping your feet pressed back as you lean forwards. Take this gently, as your inner thighs will be pretty tight after all that skiing.
• Stretches inner thighs.

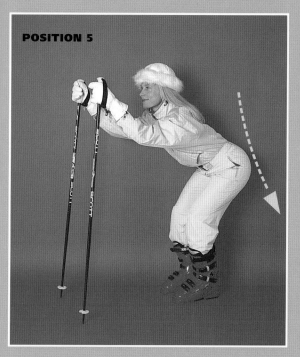

POSITION 5

## POSITION 5: MOBILIZER

**Good for getting you used to the position for downhill slopes.**

**BEFORE YOU SKI:** Bend into this position and straighten again 8 times.

**FOR YOUR APRÈS-SKI:** Bend and straighten 6 times.
• Use the ski poles for balance, so that you can bend with the weight towards the heels. Keep the back straight and the abdominals pulled up.

## POSITION 1: STRETCH

**Good for all the basic moves in dance and gym.**

Get into this position by sitting on both knees first, and then extending one leg straight back behind you, pressing that hip well into the floor. Then bend the back leg up so that you can pull the foot in toward your back.

**BEFORE YOUR PRACTICE SESSION:** Hold for 20 seconds each leg.

**AFTER YOUR PRACTICE SESSION:** Hold for 30 seconds each way then release and pummel the thighs.
• Stretches front of thighs and front of hips and gives a little flex to the lower back.

POSITION 1

## POSITION 2A AND 2B: STRETCHES

**Shown here are two positions that are good for flexing the lower back. The first is more usual in dance, the second in gymnastics. Unless you are flexible, take great care.**

**BEFORE YOUR PRACTICE SESSION:** Hold for 10 seconds and repeat 5 times.

**AFTER YOUR PRACTICE SESSION:** Hold for 20 seconds, and then roll the body into a ball, hugging the knees into the chest, and roll backwards and forwards to massage the lower back. Repeat 3 times.
• Stretches the abdomen area and mobilizes the lower back.

POSITION 2A AND 2B

## POSITION 3: MOBILIZER

**Good for getting your legs and back ready for action!**

Start in an upright, perfect-posture position (see Chapter 1). Reach the hands out to the side for balance, or hold onto something solid with one hand and lower the body slowly forwards. Keep your legs as straight as you can and the weight over the toes not the heels. Drop your head towards your knees and sweep your hand all the way to the floor so that it just touches, then pull in on the abdominal muscles and curl the body back to the upright position.

**BEFORE YOUR PRACTICE SESSION:** Repeat the movement 3 times very slowly and with control.

**AFTER YOUR PRACTICE SESSION:** As above.
• Mobilizes and stretches the backs of the legs and lower back.

POSITION 3

## POSITION 4: MOBILIZER

**Good for warming up the hips for fast, high kicks.**

Move the bent knee in a figure 8 shape, forwards and backwards. Keep the standing leg bent and hold onto something to keep your balance!

**BEFORE YOUR PRACTICE SESSION:** Repeat the movement 8 times on each side.

**AFTER YOUR PRACTICE:** Repeat the movement 4 times, very slowly and with control.
• Mobilizes the hips.

POSITION 4

## POSITION 5: STRETCH

**Do this only if you are feeling flexible. See page 107 for a detailed description of how best to get into the splits.**

**Good for making the legs even more flexible.**

Start by adopting the lunge position, with hands on the floor for support. Now gently slide your back leg away from you, taking your back foot as far away from the front one as it will go. Only go as low as is comfortable. If you go a little lower each time you will see improve-

ment very quickly, and this is a good way to see just how flexible you are becoming.

**BEFORE YOUR PRACTICE SESSION:** Hold for 10 seconds each leg.

**AFTER YOUR PRACTICE:** Hold for 30 seconds each way, then release and gently rub the groin area with your hands.
• Stretches groin, legs and inner thighs.

POSITION 5

POSITION 6

## POSITION 6: STRETCH

**Good for rapid movements and extreme stretch moves required in gymnastics.**

Start with legs as wide as possible and, with hands on the floor, slide the palms out as far as you can.

**BEFORE YOUR PRACTICE SESSION:** Hold for 30 seconds.

**AFTER YOUR PRACTICE:** Hold for 30 seconds each way, then release and lightly pummel the groin and inner thighs with your fists.
• Stretches groin, legs and inner thighs.

## POSITION 1: MOBILIZER

**Good for loosening the upper body muscles.**

Move the elbow in a full circular motion first one way then the other. Make sure the elbow describes every part of the circle as you move it smoothly.

**BEFORE YOUR RUN:** Perform 8-10 times and repeat with other arm.

**AFTER YOUR RUN:** Perform more slowly 6-8 times.
• Mobilizes the arm and shoulder area.

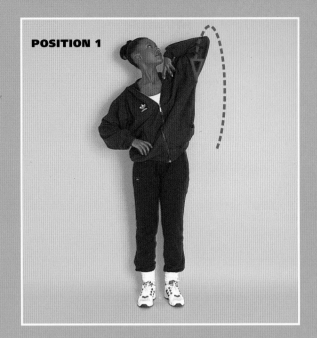

POSITION 1

## POSITION 2: STRETCH

**Good for running, jumping and speed sports.**

Seated in the position shown in the photo reach forwards as far as you can over your straight leg.

**BEFORE YOUR RUN/WALK:** Hold for 20 seconds and repeat on each leg.

**AFTER YOUR RUN/WALK:** Hold for 30 seconds and repeat on each leg.
• Stretches the hamstring and calf as well as the buttock and side of the bent thigh.

POSITION 2

## POSITION 3: MOBILIZER

**Good for all running and walking actions of the legs.**

Here you are simply swinging the arms as you push off the foot to effect a light jogging movement.

**BEFORE YOUR RUN/WALK:** Jog lightly 10-15 times.

**AFTER YOUR RUN/WALK:** Jog lightly 10-15 times.
• Mobilizes the legs, feet and ankles.

POSITION 3

POSITION 4

## POSITION 4: STRETCH

**Good for all running and walking actions of the legs.**

Take a small lunge position here, but put the emphasis on feeling the stretch in the back of the calf on the back leg.

**BEFORE YOUR RUN/WALK:** Hold for 20-30 seconds and repeat on each leg.

**AFTER YOUR RUN/WALK:** Hold for 20-30 seconds and repeat on each leg.
• Stretches the calf and Achilles tendon (which will stretch slightly).

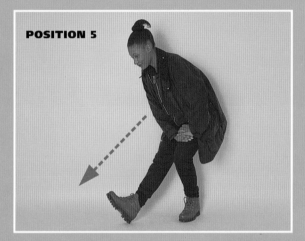

POSITION 5

## POSITION 5: STRETCH

**Good for all running and walking actions of the legs and helps prevent cramp and injury to the back of the legs.**

Adopt the position as shown in the photo with hands resting on the bent knee for support. Press forward to feel the stretch up the back of the leg.

**BEFORE YOUR RUN/WALK:** Hold for 20-30 seconds.

**AFTER YOUR RUN/WALK:** Hold for 20-30 seconds and repeat on each leg.
• Stretches the hamstrings.

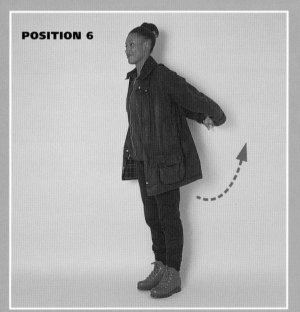

POSITION 6

## POSITION 6: MOBILIZER

**Ensures arms are mobilized for sudden or reaching actions.**

Lift the arms behind you as high as you can to mobilize the shoulder joints.

**BEFORE YOUR RUN/WALK:** Lift as high as you can, and lower with a brief hold 15 times.

**AFTER YOUR RUN/WALK:** Lift and hold for longer, even tipping your arms right over your head (and bending the knees) to really increase the stretch (see page 42).
• Mobilizes the shoulders and arm area.

# ballistic stretch

Ballistic stretching means "bouncing" from an initial stretch position in order to increase the stretch further. Some sports use ballistic-style movements as a substantial part of their repertoire. The kicks, head and back-flicks made by dancers, the jumps and whips of the gymnast and the explosive punch-kicks of the martial artist, all call upon lightning speed extension of the muscles. In these sports then, it is essential to put the body through some of these fast movements in the warm-up phase to prevent injury.

## SOME BAD REVIEWS

In recent years, the ballistic stretching method has received a lot of bad press in the fitness world. As many physiotherapists point out, there are various problems with this approach:
• Any rapid stretch without warning will activate the stretch reflex (see page 22) and make the muscle tense up rather than encouraging it to release.
• Rapid bouncing, using your body weight, may take the movement out of control, so that it is difficult to stop the movement before any damage occurs. What happens then is that small tears (micro trauma) occur that can lead to a build-up of scar tissue. This, in turn, may ultimately lead to less flexible muscles – the exact opposite of what you are aiming for!

## ON THE PLUS SIDE

On the "pro" side, some physiotherapists suggest that:
• If you do ballistic movements in a gentle, controlled way, you can retrain the stretch reflex so that it doesn't occur while you are doing the movement.
• Some ballistic-style movements also provide the body with speed and mobility. For example, leg swings allow the legs to mobilize and stretch a little at the same time.

## 'ROCK' NOT 'SHOCK'

Ballistic stretching – a certain amount of moving within a position to push the stretch a little further or simply to become comfortable with the stretch you are in – can have benefits.

Take, for example, a stretch position for the inner thighs where you are sitting with your legs straight and out to the side, and you wish to reach further over one leg and then into the middle. Rather than going straight into the full stretch over one leg, it is far better to start by rocking the body from side to side. This is similar to a certain mobilizing exercise, where the body is given a warning in the areas about to be used and there is some build-up of heat in the hip joints. Similarly, when starting to stretch forwards, if you put your hands on the floor in front of you and rock gently backwards and forwards, these little pressing movements will warm up the inner thighs before you push as far forwards as you can go.

## TAKING IT FURTHER

With this type of stretching, once you stretch to your initial limit, you can then do some more gentle rocking to help you become used to that position – and eventually you may go a bit further. The thing to remember when rocking or doing little pushes is that your hands should always be on the floor to support you as a safe-guard against going too far. In this way you are always in control. Used carefully and correctly, these gentle rocking movements can really help your body acclimatize to the stretch and distract your mind so that the stretch can be maintained. (See Chapters 2 and 4 for more on exactly how to stretch.)

At all times do try and remember that stretching is a gradual process and that no amount of forcing, bouncing or bending will stretch the muscles in one session. In fact if you push things too far you are prone to over stretching and thus "pulling" or even tearing a muscle. Always work slowly and conscientiously toward your stretch goals, making the process a regular event rather than a forced one-off session.

## CHECK IT OUT

If you find you are very stiff or that over the course of weeks your stretch ability is not improving it may be worth a trip to the physiotherapist just to check there are no anatomical restrictions or other conditions that may be limiting you. Young, as well as older people can suffer from various forms of arthritis which tends to cause undue stiffness in the joints and if this were to be the case then your physio might even recommend some gentle stretches to help the condition. Most people, however, need nothing more than a regular stretch programme worked into their lives.

## THE BEST PROGRAMME

Throughout this book there have been many different methods of stretching detailed. It is up to you to try as many ways as you can and find the ones which work best for you. People who have come from competitive sports background, particularly those in martial arts, gymnastics and dance will be accustomed to stretching in a somewhat ballistic mode and this may be the method that appeals to them most. Their bodies will be used to the feelings of stretch and they will have learned how far they can go.

Others who are less familiar with the whole concept of stretching may find any kind of stretch very painful at first. This is because the body is feeling something unfamiliar and it will take time for the body and mind to relax with the sensations and learn not too panic. That is why a gradual build-up is such a good idea. It is also a good idea to use the different methods of stretch at different times. If you are feeling full of energy and raring to go one morning, you may want to make your session more dynamic by adopting stretch positions and moving around in them to really become at ease. You may also be in the mood to try the moving sequences in Chapter 6 which give you the opportunity to make your stretch programme a fun and creative experience! These kinds of stretches are also good to do with children. On the other hand if you are just starting to move in this way again, after a long break or an injury then the levelled programmes will help you progress along with the relaxation stretches in Chapter 6. Relaxing in a stretch position will allow your body to learn that stretch need not be painful or awkward, but can help relieve stiffness in a non-threatening way. If you have worked hard for a week or so and your body is feeling a little jaded use some of the partner stretches to re-enthuse yourself and make the session really fun! Then get your partner to try out some of the massage techniques mentioned to entirely relax those muscles!

# CHAPTER 5 stretching with a PARTNER

This chapter is all about stretching with a friend. There are many ways that two people can work together to bring variety to their stretch routines and increase their stretching potential as they do so. Working with a partner can help you stay motivated longer and have fun at the same time!

Sometimes it can be difficult to get your body into certain stretch positions. A partner can help in this process, acting rather as a personal instructor would, by checking the body position, guiding a limb to its correct placement, and ensuring that there are no jerky movements and so less risk of injury. They can also provide some massage and a post-stretch rub down – which always feels better when it is done by someone else!

## DO'S AND DON'TS

When stretching with a partner, there are some important safety points that must be noted:

Communication is vital when you are working with someone else's body. Remember, you cannot feel what your partner is feeling – only by talking to them and listening to exactly what they say will you be able to maintain enough control. Whenever you begin to help your partner to stretch out, keep your mind on what you are doing and constantly ask them how they are feeling.

If you are the "presser", as opposed to the person being stretched, check your partner's posture before you begin and during the stretch; make sure there is not slouching or tendency to favour one side of the body. Once in a stretch position, the person being stretched is often less aware of his or her position than you will be.

The presser must also check their partner's breathing. Breathing during partner stretching should be normal and regular, with no held breaths. Occasionally, you may direct them to inhale strongly and exhale slowly, to aid the stretch. The following pages will indicate when this is appropriate.

## BODY TALK

As you practice your partner stretching techniques, you will find that you become more adept at listening, and even feeling, your partner's body signals. When you first press your partner into a position, you will feel the resistance in their muscles. As you continue to hold, and the stretch reflex becomes de-activated, you will feel a slight "give" in the muscles. To begin with, you will have to ask your partner exactly what she or he is feeling, but after a while you will start to recognize the signs – just as you learn to feel what is comfortable for your own body you will know when a muscle is releasing, when it is tiring and so on.

Remember also to check that your partner's breathing is slow and rhythmical. They should not be holding their breath – if they are then they are obviously tense and not relaxed in the position. Also, always keep talking to your partner throughout and make sure that they are talking back.

### A HELPING HAND

**Gentle manipulation of a certain area by someone else will often help to relieve superficial stiffness, discomfort or injury, and it may be that a partner can work on areas that are too difficult for you to reach properly yourself (see Chapter 6). Any major injuries such as breaks or sprains – or areas that you think may be badly injured – must, of course, be looked at by a qualified medic; don't try to act as each other's physiotherapist.**

## PARTNER STRETCHING TECHNIQUES

When starting to stretch a partner, you must understand that quite a large amount of pressure is normally needed. Most bodies are heavy – and limbs are surprisingly heavy! So when manipulating someone into a position, it is important to handle them firmly and with confidence. It is always better if the two people stretching each other are relatively similar in height and weight. If you are not, don't worry, but make sure that the heavier person takes extra care.

### THE ART OF TOUCH

Don't be afraid to touch and grasp your partner, and don't shrink from pressing firmly when the following pages indicate that is necessary. Usually, the positions where you can do this best are those where you have the ability to use your own body weight to increase your partner's stretch range.

### STAYING WITH IT

With partner stretches, the stretch needs to be maintained for some time, usually 20-50 seconds, so that the developmental phase of the stretch can be activated. This is when you feel (or your partner will tell you) that the muscle has started to release slightly. At this point, you can take the stretch a little further, allowing your weight to go over a little more as you feel your partner's muscles letting you do so. Always make sure, however, that you are in control of your own weight, and therefore have the ability to pull away from your partner if necessary.

## LETTING GO

If your partner expresses discomfort at any time, or at the end of the stretch, the way you release your partner is as important as the way you apply the pressure. Never just jump away from the stretch you have made, but withdraw gently and firmly, so that the muscle stretch releases gently too. Jumping back from pressing – for example if your partner suddenly says "ow!" – is much more likely to distress the muscle because it springs back too quickly. Always release the hold slowly. Withdraw the pressure in a slow, controlled manner, or ask your partner to press against you to start the withdrawal. In this way, your partner's muscles will have time to readjust and "understand" that the pressure has been released. Your partner may then need to take a few seconds to relax and recover. You can aid him by gently rubbing the muscles you have stretched, bringing blood and warmth to the area. Keep chatting to your partner and check that his muscles feel back to normal before embarking on the next stretch. Or swap around so that he can repeat the stretch for you before you start on him again! This gives time for each muscle group being stretched to recover.

One of the most exciting ways to stretch is to use the P.N.F. method outlined below – which really is much easier when you have a partner. Some of the stretches featured over the following pages use this method, and you will see how it really extends the limits of your stretching capabilities.

# P.N.F.
# stretching

Proprioceptive Neuro-muscular Facilitation was adapted from physiotherapy techniques for stroke patients. P.N.F. works on two principles:

**1.** If a muscle is contracted hard for at least 10-20 seconds, then immediately afterwards the tone of the muscle will decrease briefly. If a stretch is applied at this point, it will allow a greater range of motion.

**2.** That, when a muscle is contracted, the opposing muscle releases and the tone of that muscle decreases, briefly allowing a greater stretch – this is known as reciprocal inhibition.

There are two ways to carry out P.N.F. stretches – either by using the muscle in a vigorous isometric (held) position for some time, or by using the opposing muscle group in the same manner. When you release the

## A CASE IN POINT

**As a child, did you ever play the game where you stand in a doorway and push your arms against the door frame as hard as you can for a minute? Try it now. When you walk away from the door, your hands will float upwards as if they are weightless and have a mind of their own. ("Magic!" We used to exclaim as children.) This is reciprocal inhibition in action.**

hold, the sustained tension will facilitate a greater stretch. Remember when using this method that you should warm up thoroughly first. Warm muscles can contract much more, and for longer – which is necessary for this way of working – and they will stretch further afterwards.

## PUSHING FURTHER

You will find that a partner is especially helpful for the second method, giving you someone to push against initially. And when you release the pressure, you have your partner to guide your limbs through the greater range of motion that you have just gained.

This method is particularly good for areas where stiffness is a particularly stubborn problem. When you feel you really cannot go any further in a stretch or in that a particular set of muscles (the hamstrings, for example, are particularly inflexible), P.N.F. stretching can help you find new stretch in the those muscles – if done regularly and responsibly. This type of stretching will also add variety to your stretch work-out, as it concentrates the mind and works the opposing muscles, so you will be toning some of your muscles at the same time.

Turn to the following pages to try a variety of partner stretches that are fun, safe and bound to extend you!

It is possible to attempt P.N.F. stretching on your own, although it is much easier, and probably safer, to do it with a partner to guide you.

If you are on your own, try a few different ways of feeling the syndrome just to get you used to the idea. See "A Case in Point" box. Also try the following. Sit in a comfortable position, with one leg outstretched and resting on a couple of cushions or a low step. This allows the leg to be raised slightly off the floor so that you can press down with some force. Now press the foot down towards the floor as if you were trying to push it through the cushions! Maintain this tension for 30–50 seconds. Be careful not to push through the back of the knee too much. You should not feel the back of the knee being stressed, so try to keep the tension in the quadriceps (front of thigh muscles). Now release the tensions and, taking hold of the working leg, roll onto your back and pull the straight leg in towards your nose as far as it will go. Hold momentarily and then release. Roll back to an upright sitting position to repeat the process again. If you repeat this three times, you should notice a distinct increase in how far your leg can be pulled towards your nose from the time you started to the time you finished. Repeat the whole process regularly for lasting benefit.

# 1. THE BRIDGE

Have your partner sit comfortably, with the soles of his feet touching each other and legs bent, with knees falling out to the side. The feet don't need to be pulled in tightly towards the groin but should be placed quite far out in front, so that he is relaxed. Your partner should sit with a straight back, lifting up through the spine from the hips, and take a deep breath in and then one out.

Position yourself directly behind your partner, sitting high up on your knees, so that, when force is required, you are in a position to apply it. Now the person being stretched should place his hands on his ankles – not around his feet – and relax his back so that he curls slightly forwards. With your right

**POSITION 1: THE BRIDGE**

hand, press firmly on his lower back and with the flat of your hand try to press your partner further forwards from the base of his spine. You will probably find that your partner does not move very far. Although this is where stretches should begin, most people need pressure further up the spine to help them bend.

Next, take your left hand and press the middle of your partner's back to apply pressure gently but firmly, easing them a little further forwards. Finally, still maintaining the pressure, place both hands wherever the back is highest – it should still be curved – and press firmly with both hands until your partner tells you he has reached his conformable limit.

Once you have reached this position, hold for 20-30 seconds. Now ask your partner to press his back against your palms as if to push you upwards. Resist the push for several seconds and then gently allow your partner to press himself to sitting and recover. After this stretch, let your partner bring his knees together and, sitting with his hands behind for support, have him tip his knees from one side to the other to help him recover from the sustained pressure.

## THE PRESSER

While you are exerting pressure on your partner, be very aware of how he might be feeling. Talk to him, particularly as you push him over, and ask if he is comfortable. If you feel, during the 30-second hold, that your partner's muscles have relaxed, then go with this and take your pressure lower as his muscles allow you to. Once you have gone lower, however, don't allow your partner to lift up again. Hold it there. Never force your partner lower than you feel his muscles will allow.

At the end of some of the following stretches, you may need to help your partner come back to the original position. Or try asking him to push against you, which will signal to his muscles that the stretch has ended. Take a few moments to allow your partner to recover and move around to release tension.

## THE STRETCHEE

It is very important to try and relax your muscles and to have faith in your partner to stretch you out responsibly and with delicate care. If you don't trust your partner, you will not be able to relax fully and get the greatest benefit from such a programme.

Take slow, deep breaths and concentrate on telling your muscles not to fight the pressure but to r-e-l-e-a-s-e. As well as talking to your partner and keeping her informed of what you are feeling, you also need to have your own internal dialogue going to encourage and reassure your own body! In this way your brain will learn to let your muscles release without fear of injury.

## SAFTEY FIRST

**If, at any time, you feel your partner is pushing you too far, try using these code words:**

- **"HOLD", telling your partner to maintain the stretch.**
- **"ENOUGH", telling your partner to withdraw pressure slowly and gently.**

**Above all, don't panic when you feel the stretch reflex activate and the muscles initially tighten and pull away. Keep communicating with your partner, and with yourself, breathe deeply, and remind yourself that you will soon become accustomed to the sensation.**

## 2. THE MAGIC LAMP

This stretch uses the second P.N.F. method of stretching described earlier in this chapter (page 85).

### METHOD

Basically, the principle here is to use your partner's resistance to allow you to push hard with the top of your thigh so that your Quadriceps muscles are in a strong contraction for some seconds. When you release the back of the leg, the hamstring muscle will be that much more supple. If you repeat this stretch pattern up to three times on each leg, you will really notice the difference in the stretch you have obtained; from the time you start to the time you complete the last movement.

### THE STRETCHEE

The person being stretched stands with her back to a wall and presses her heels and bottom in tight to that wall. Place the hands either side to aid balance. Now bend your leg and lift your foot off the floor to "give" one leg to your partner. Allow your partner to lift that leg as high as it will go naturally. You should not feel that he is forcing it at this stage, you should simply feel that he has lifted it to its natural limit. Make sure that your other foot is flat on the ground, your bottom is not being pulled away from the wall, and your stomach is not sagging.

Now take a deep breath in and, as you exhale, start to exert force with your lifted leg, trying to force it down towards the ground. Use the muscles on the top of the thigh – look at these muscles, concentrate on them and press as hard as you can for 50

seconds. If you are pressing hard enough, your partner should have a hard time keeping that leg up there!

Make sure you don't feel too much of a push through the joint of the knee. Try to keep the pressing leg just very slightly bent and concentrate on using the quadriceps to exert force. Keep breathing at all times while your partner counts out 50 seconds. When he tells you to release, stop pushing immediately and just allow your limb to be lifted.

### THE PRESSER

The presser starts by holding his partner's leg in both hands and lifting it as far as it will naturally go. Bend your knees and pull in on the stomach to give yourself support – once there is pressure on that leg you will find it really hard work!

Now time 50 seconds on your stopwatch and hold your partner's leg where it is, as she pushes downwards. Don't try to lift the leg any higher – simply resist her attempts to push it down to the floor. Keep both arms bent as you resist the push, so that you are taking the weight in your arms and not in the spine. After 50 seconds, ask her to release. As you feel the pushing cease, wait 5 seconds and then gently lift the leg 2-3 inches higher.

You should now find that the leg will lift a few extra inches quite effortlessly. Don't push it any further than this but simply take the leg to its new natural height and ask your partner to start pushing again. Repeat the process two more times, followed by a gentle lift each time to extend the muscle. Repeat on the other leg and then swap roles.

By the end of the stretch, your leg

will probably have gone from, say, a 90-degree angle to one of 110 degrees. This is where the use of the quadriceps has allowed a greater stretch to take place in the opposing muscles – in this case the hamstrings. Because many people experience stiff legs, this is a really good stretch to help extend your flexibility. It is particularly useful to be working with a partner because lifting your own leg into a position it doesn't want to reach is pretty difficult.

Remember, to capitalize on the increased flexibility you have gained, you must repeat this process often. In this way the legs get used to stretching and the flexibility will last.

As you feel your flexibility increasing with this method, you can go on to try other stretches with your legs. Try the splits practice on page 107, as you should now find this easier and may get lower than when you first attempted it. In addition, remember that the Magic Lamp stretch can also be used to lift the legs to the side, so that you are stretching the adductor muscles as well. Perform the same sequence as in the main example, but stand with the side of your body pressed to the wall and have your partner lift the leg in a forward diagonal. The leg should lift to the side, without hitching the hip up.

You could also try a similar P.N.F. stretch where you are seated with your legs open and touching your partner's (see picture on page 91). In this position, you would squeeze in with both your legs and then release and allow your partner to ease your legs outwards.

**POSITION 3: THE ROWBOAT**

## 3. THE ROWBOAT

This stretch allows both partners to stretch out the other person's inner thigh muscles with enough force to make a difference, but with as little risk of injury as possible.

**STARTING POSITION**

Both partners sit on the floor facing one another and with their feet out as far to each side as is naturally comfortable. The presser places her feet against her partner's ankles and keeps her knees bent. Then the presser supports herself with her hands behind her and straightens her legs by pushing the legs of her partner further outwards. Now stretchee and presser join hands, grasping each other's wrists securely.

this lean for 15-20 seconds and then lean forwards and allow your partner to lean back himself, feeling the stretch in your own thighs. Hold for just a few seconds and then lean backwards once more on your side.

## THE STRETCHEE

As your partner leans back, allow yourself to be pulled forwards and feel the stretch in your inner thighs. Keep your back as straight as possible and keep the stomach lifted so that there is no pulling on your lower or upper back. If you feel you are being pulled too far, use the code words "hold" or "enough" to give yourself you a breather before you try again. As you hold the stretch position, breathe normally and try to relax the legs as they are stretched. When your partner eases forwards, use this as your cue to pull gently with your arms and then start to lean backwards – not too far – to give your partner a gentle stretch.

With one partner as the stretchee, rock gently back wards and forwards 3 times before resting and swapping roles. When you wish to change roles, remember to change the foot position so that one person is being stretched further than the other. Try to do this stretch together as part of your regular stretch programme. (If you don't always have a partner, you can try doing the same sort of stretch by pushing your feet against the wall and leaning towards it).

After the stretch, bring your legs together. Now gently massage both of your inner thighs with your palms, or lightly pummel the muscles there to bring the blood to these areas and so relieve any tension there may be.

## THE PRESSER

Now, holding onto your partner's arms securely and keeping your stomach well lifted and your back straight, start to lean backwards slowly, pulling your partner towards you gently. Use your arm strength to ease your partner towards you.

Keep talking to your partner the whole time, so that you know how much of a stretch he is feeling. As you lean backwards, you stretch your partner's inner thighs, while keeping his legs stable with your feet. Hold

## 4. COBRACATION

This is a great stretch for the arms, chest and shoulders, as well as helping to flex the lower back area, which is an important part to keep mobile.

### THE STRETCHEE

The person being stretched lies face down on the floor and folds her arms, pressing her head through her arms to rest on the floor. Your partner will then pick you up by holding your arms and gently pulling them towards him.

You will feel a stretch around the shoulders and chest as your head falls forwards to hang below your arms and your arms are stretched back. You will also feel a bend in the lower back. All of these feelings should be pleasant. Nothing should be feeling as if it is being pulled too far. If you do experience any discomfort, then use the safety code words. Keep breathing naturally the whole time you are in the stretch position and think about relaxing your spine. To get your body used to this stretch, you may need to try it once, release it, and then repeat it again.

### THE LIFTER

Stand with feet apart and knees well bent as you reach down to lift your partner. Slide your hands gently beneath the upper arms, nearest the elbow joints, and once you have a good hold, gently lift her upper body upwards and back, towards you. Take care not to pinch the soft flesh of this area as you pick her up and arch her back slowly upwards. (Make sure you're checking that she is alright.)

When you are satisfied that she is comfortable, rest your bent arms on your knees. In this way the position is stable and the weight of her body is taken by your legs, and not by your back.

Hold the stretch for just 15-20 seconds and then gently release her to the floor. Be aware that her forehead is the first thing to touch the floor, so lower her gently and with control. Gently massage her shoulders to help the muscles recover.

Don't forget to swap partners so that the other person gets a chance to be stretched. There is no reason why two people of differing weights cannot perform this exercise together; just remember that, when the lighter person is lifting, certain rules are carefully observed (see box Protect Your Back).

### PROTECT YOUR BACK

Whenever you are lifting something heavy, protect your lower back by:
• Always bending the knees and squatting down – to 90° only or just below – with the weight over the heels and the knees behind the toes.
• Pulling in on the stomach muscles and the pelvic floor muscles to support your internal organs.
• Pulling the object or person in close to you, if possible, with the strength in your arms.
• As you lift, pressing through the legs and buttocks to use the large muscles in these areas to lift the weight of the object or person. The upper body should be fairly upright.
• Remembering that you should never "hinge" from the back – always press through the legs.

# 5. THE THIN EDGE OF THE WEDGE

This is a gentle stretch exercise that is excellent for stretching out and relaxing the shoulders and neck. It is especially good after a long, hard day or if you feel that your back is tight or have a headache.

## THE PRESSEE

Have your partner sit comfortably in front of you, with her back straight and stomach pulled in. Now, using a very gentle touch and communicating all the time, work your way through the following sequence.

Place your right hand in front around the bottom of the throat, on the very uppermost part of the breastbone, and ease her back towards you, so that her weight is supported against your body. Now place the other hand on top of her head, pushing it gently downwards. You should feel that your two hands are pushing in opposite directions. One hand is keeping the spine tall while the other stretches the muscles at the back of the neck.

Now gently move your hand from the top of the head and, if possible, use it to grip her hair (not too tightly!) and pull her head into an upright position. Using the hair means that your partner doesn't have to use her neck muscles at all to lift her head, so that she can keep them as relaxed as possible.

Once upright, place your right hand on the left side of her head and your left hand on her left shoulder. Very, very gently press down with the hand that is on the shoulder while the other hand guides the head over to the side (see photo). Your partner will feel a stretch down the left side of her neck.

Do not hold this stretch for more than 10 seconds and again use the hair to lift the head back to an upright position. Now reverse hand positions to repeat the stretch on the other side of her neck and finish by lifting her head so that it is upright.

Afterwards, you may wish to repeat the back-of-the-neck stretch once more and then gently place your fingers and thumbs across the back of the shoulders and massage gently. Finally, place the first two fingers of each of your hands on the sides of the neck and massage in small circles up the sides of the neck and down again.

## THE STRETCHEE

The stretchee should really enjoy this stretch, which will take the tension out of her neck and the top of her shoulders. But do let your partner know if you feel that his touch is too hard at any time. And don't forget to swap actions!

### SAFETY NOTES

• **Don't press heavily on the side of her head. The head is very heavy – up to 12lb in weight – and although the neck muscles are used to supporting this weight they are still relatively thin and can easily be pulled. This is why mobilizing the neck is always a good idea (see Chapter 6).**
• **In fact, you don't need to exert pressure in this stretch at all. Simply keep the hand on the shoulder to stop it from lifting up and use your other hand to guide the head to one side.**

**POSITION 5: THIN EDGE OF THE WEDGE**

# 6. THE BACK RELEASER

This final partner sequence is not so much a stretch as a mobilizer and relaxer for the spine. One partner must give the complete weight of her legs to the other so that they can be supported and moved gently in any direction. This suspends any tension and weight that was pressing down on the lower back, bringing real relief. The process is so relaxing that it has to be felt to be believed and the only problem will be getting your partner off the floor to return the compliment!

## THE PRESSEE

Stand above your partner, with your legs well bent in the squat position, and lift your partner's legs off the floor. Lift the feet only a foot or so off the ground and keep them at this height as you move them around.

Be careful of your back – a totally relaxed person has very heavy legs. Keep your knees bent with your stomach lifted for support and use the muscles in the arms to lift the legs.

## NOW PERFORM THESE ACTIONS:

**1.** Keeping the feet level, lift the ankles gently up and down (only by about 5-8 cm).
**2.** Lift one leg and then the other, as if the legs were walking.
**3.** Bring the ankles together and move them in a circle, 2-3 times each way.
**4.** Gently shake the legs to check that your partner is relaxing her limbs fully.
**5.** Lift both feet and legs all the way up, walking your own feet forwards, until the soles of your partner's feet are facing the ceiling. At this point, you should feel the legs start to bend. Gently pull them straight and walk your feet back out again so that you lower her legs to a position that is just off the floor once more. Repeat this walk-in 2 or 3 times and, as you lower the legs for the last time, gently stretch the legs so that your partner experiences a mild traction (pull) as you relax her lower back.
**6.** Walk the legs all the way to one side, so that your partner's body now forms an L shape (like a side-

### POSITION 6: BACK RELEASER

#### DO'S AND DON'TS

**The stretchee must make sure that her legs are completely 'heavy' and relaxed. The pressee must keep knees bent and use the muscles in the arms to support the weight.**

ways bend), and then repeat on the other side so that she also feels a stretch up the sides of the torso. Bring her legs gently back to centre.

**7.** To finish, hold both the ankles and shake them gently so that the shake goes up the length of her entire body before replacing her feet lightly on the floor.

**8.** Get your partner to roll over onto her side and then push herself up to a seated position to bring herself back slowly to a fully alert state.

Once she has recovered, she has to perform the same hard work for you!

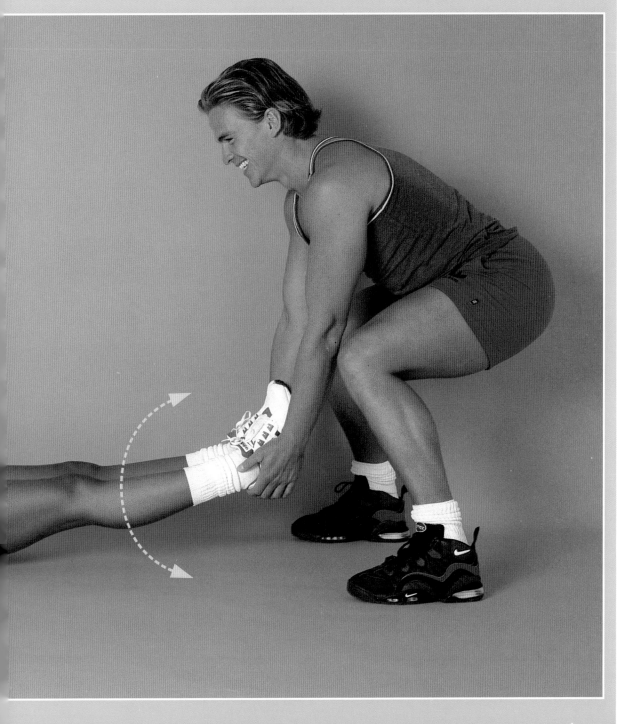

# 6 CHAPTER keep STRETCHING

Stretching is important not only as part of a well-planned work-out routine, but also as an activity by itself. Stretching sessions will keep you supple and feeling as if you can move without hindrance or pain. If you are exercising your body hard, and particularly if you are building up your muscles, then stretching is a must to keep your flexibility and range of movement. And as you get older, stretching should become an even more important aspect of maintaining flexibility in order to stay active.

## GET MOVING

Stretching is also a good way to reintroduce the body to exercise and fitness. If you are recovering from an injury, or even just a long period of inactivity, then a little stretching will get you moving again. Even those of us who are motivated to work out regularly can have periods where illness, work or family pressures disrupt our normal fitness regime, and stretching is one of the most pleasurable ways to re-introduce the body to movement. Throughout this book there are stretches that chal-

lenge the body as well as being pleasurable and helping to motivate you.

## STRETCH AND CHILDBIRTH

After the birth of a baby is a particularly good time to start a gentle stretch programme. You will find that it will revitalize the body and get it moving in ways that it has not been used to for quite a while. Over the following pages there is a selection of ante-natal and postnatal stretches designed to keep you supple all the way through and after your pregnancy.

## ILLNESSES AND INJURY

During your recovery after an injury or illness is another particularly good time to introduce some stretch sequences to your body. You may have been immobile for a while or a part of you may simply be stiff from lack of use, so turn to any of the stretches in this book that you feel will get that area moving.

## PROBLEM SOLVING

This chapter also features stretches and mobilizers for problem areas – areas where many people experience stiffness or lack of mobility. Pages 106-111 deal with stretches for the back, legs, neck and shoulders and suggest ways to mobilize and stretch these often stubborn areas.

If you haven't been moving athletically for some time, for whatever reason, then muscles and joints will

tighten up and you will feel stiffer than you did when you were exercising regularly. This is because muscles, ligaments and tendons all tighten slightly with lack of use and it takes regular "encouragement" sessions to get the synovial fluid lubricating the joints fully once again and the body

used to moving in certain ways. It also takes time for the mind to get used to not overreacting to the stretch reflex.

Always start with short, gentle sessions of stretch and mobilizing exercises to encourage and reaccustom the body to exercise. Remember that when you first start, you may

experience some stiffness the following day, so take things gradually. Along with stretching and mobilizing stiff areas you may also like to try some gentle massage techniques to help relieve tension and discomfort in sore muscles. You will find some suggestions on the following page.

## MASSAGE

Massage is an excellent way of helping the muscles of the body to relax. A full, all-over body massage should be given by a qualified therapist who knows the basic pressure points and ways of relieving them. Gently rubbing and cajoling a stiff area, however, is something anyone can do either for themselves or for their partner.

If you have stretched a certain area it can feel particularly good to gently rub, knead or pound the muscle, bringing blood back to the surface and creating some warmth. In the same way, if an area feels sore or stiff, lightly squeeze the muscles between thumb and fingers and knead along the line of the muscle to warm it and get it used to some movement.

Healthy muscles can easily be grasped and kneaded and should feel malleable and pliable without too many lumps or knots just below the surface. If you come across an area where your partner cries out with discomfort, you may need to spend some extra time on this region, gently pressing and kneading around the sore spot to release the tension. End your massage session with some light tapping (with cupped hands) or pounding to get the blood flowing through the area once again.

### CRAMPS

When you are feeling stiff or under tension you can sometimes experience cramps. Cramping is not fully understood, although it is thought to be a lack of calcium or possibly other minerals. What does seem certain, however, is that we are particularly

### SELF HELP FOR CRAMP

**If cramping occurs, try not to panic but immediately press with the heels of both hands on the area that you feel is in spasm. Pressing down on the contracted muscle will encourage it to flatten and relax its grip. As you feel the muscle release, you can then start to stretch the muscle, which will help to prevent the cramp reoccurring immediately.**

prone to it at certain times of our lives – during periods of stress or during pregnancy, for example.

What happens with cramp is that the muscle contracts very strongly and stays contracted in a spasm, bringing sudden and alarming discomfort to the sufferer.

### AIDING RECOVERY

Cramp can often leave the muscle feeling sore, so gentle rubbing, or even the application of some heat, can help the muscle recover. If you know you are prone to cramp, then regular stretching and massage of the area can really help. Pregnant women, for example, often experience cramp in their feet and calves at night, so a gentle pre-sleep stretch could be a good idea. See page 105 for full directions.

### INJURY

Injuries usually need proper medical attention and lots of rest, but once you have taken advice, a gentle treatment of heat and cold can sometimes help to relieve any soreness or discomfort. If you have a sore or

overworked muscle, then warming the area up is a must before you try to use it again. A gentle warm-up (as detailed in Chapter 1) and gentle massage around the area can help to bring blood to the sore area and prepare it for use.

There are also many products available on the market which warm the area. These are a good idea if used in moderation and as an extra – not as a substitute for proper warm-up exercises. Cold sprays are also available and these can help take the sting out of sore muscles after a work-out. Do not use cold sprays before a work-out, as these can numb the muscles and you need to be able to feel discomfort so that you know when you are overdoing things. Remember, pain is usually there for a reason and it is not advisable to ignore it or use a substance that might mask it.

At all times, do try and remember that stretching is a gradual process and that no amount of forcing, bouncing or stretching will stretch the muscles in one session. In fact, if you push things too far, you will be prone to overstretching and thus "pulling" or even tearing a muscle. Always work slowly and conscientiously towards your stretch goals, making the process a regular event rather than a forced, one-off session.

### A VISIT TO THE PHYSIOTHERAPIST

If you find you are very stiff or that, over the course of several weeks, your stretch ability is not improving, it may be worth a trip to the physiotherapist, just to check that there are no anatomical restrictions or other conditions that may be limiting you.

# OTHER TIMES TO STRETCH

Remember, you can always find new opportunities to stretch if you look fot them! Stretch and mobilization exercises can help you throughout your week to keep the body ticking over and in good working order. In his book *Beirut Hostage* John McCarthy wrote in detail of the basic exercise programme that helped to keep his spirits up when he was held in captivity.

## AEROPLANE PLANS

Long plane flights are a common situation where some gentle mobilization exercises will help keep you feeling more alert and less jet-lagged at the end of your journey.

• For instance, from time to time throughout the flight, try rotating your ankles first one way and then the other. Repeat 5 or 6 times at one go.

• This will keep the ankles supple and help to encourage the blood flow through the legs – this can get sluggish when we sit in confined spaces for long periods of time.

• You can also repeat a similar action with the hands, rotating them at the wrists and stretching and bending the fingers.

• If you have enough room, try reaching up to the ceiling with both arms, stretching up as high as you can and lifting the weight upwards, off the spine.

• Breathe in deeply as you reach up and breathe out as you bring your arms down.

## TV AND BOOK BENDING

Even while you are watching TV or reading a book, don't miss out on the opportunity to get a little stretching in!

• You could take both legs out to the side (see photo on page 37) and rest your elbows on the floor (if you can) and then rest your head on your hands as you watch your favourite TV show!

• Or you could sit with one leg bent and the other leg straight (see page 78) and lean forwards as you read your book, relaxing into the stretch on one leg.

• Don't forget to swap legs at the end of each chapter.

## WATER WORKOUT

Even in the bath you can fit in the odd stretch! Your muscles will be nice and warm and relaxed so even though there isn't much room it could be a good place to stretch!

• Lie on your back and bend up one leg so that you can take hold of the ankle. Then try to straighten the leg toward you. As you get stretchier you should be able to pull the let close to the wall behind your head!

• Always make sure your free foot is braced on the end of the bath so that you don't disappear under the water!

## BUSMAN'S HOLIDAY

Even on a bus (or other mode of transport) if you find your back is feeling a little stiff from lack of movement or being curved for too long – give your body a break by placing your hands firmly on your knees. Now brace your arms as you press the top of your head towards the ceiling as far as you can while pressing your coccyx (end most part of the spine) down towards the seat. Breathe out as you press downwards and feel the spine release and extend. You can also do this exercise at home lying on your back with your legs at right angles over a bed or chair – this will really help stretch out the back.

Using these suggestions should give you the idea that you can use any activity as an opportunity to stretch – so don't miss out! – mobilize!

# antenatal
# stretching

With a growing baby inside you, it is vital to keep supple. As you increase in size, there is obviously some loss of flexibility, while tiredness and other problems tend to make you want to move around less. If you can manage some gentle stretch sessions in your working week, then this will help you to stay mobile for as long as possible and relieve some of the aches and pains of a long pregnancy.

## SAFETY AND HORMONES

By the time the baby is beginning to show (around 3-4 months), a hormone called Relaxin is well established. Relaxin affects all the connective tissue of the body – for example, the joints, joint capsules, tendons and ligaments. The purpose of relaxin is to relax all the ligaments and muscles surrounding the pelvis in order to allow the baby to pass through the narrow opening.

In non-pregnant women, the tough connective tissue known as ligaments is supple but firm and will only stretch a small amount, to allow the joints to work within their natural range. In pregnancy, with the presence of Relaxin (more pronounced in second and third pregnancies), the affected ligaments may allow the joints to go beyond their normal range. This could cause damage to the joints or allow nerves to become trapped.

This means that great care must be taken when stretching during pregnancy. Only hold stretches for eight to ten seconds. This ensures that there is no developmental stage to your stretches and that you keep well within your normal range.

## GETTING COMFORTABLE

As your pregnancy progresses, you will find certain stretch positions very uncomfortable. Lying on your front is obviously out once your stomach begins to protrude, and lying on your back is not recommended after week 20 because it can cause faintness. Trying to take hold of a foot or leg or reaching forwards to pick something up can also be difficult. The rule is – simply use the positions that are most comfortable for you. Don't stay in any one position too long and keep the legs close together as you change from one pose to another.

## POSITION 1:

Sitting on the floor with your legs open enough to facilitate your bump, slowly walk the arms forwards until you feel a gentle stretch on the back of the legs and inner thighs. Hold for 8-10 seconds only and then walk your hands back in.
• Keep the back straight and the hands on the floor for support.
• Keep your breathing as natural and regular as possible.

• You can straighten the legs and extend the feet, but don't over-point the toes as this could lead to cramp.
• Repeat this stretch two or three times.
• While you are in this position you should also remember to do your pelvic floor exercises!

## POSITION 2:

Rest your hands on something solid and, keeping a slight bend in the knees, let the back straighten and the head fall through between the arms.
• You will feel a stretching and releasing sensation in the lower back, which is very relaxing for pregnant mums, where the weight of the foetus can bear down on the lower back curve if posture is not absolutely perfect.
• You may also feel a stretch in the shoulders, where the arms are extended.
• Don't allow the stomach to sag downwards in this position and the back to arch; keep the back as straight, and as supported by the stomach muscles, as possible.
• Keep breathing regularly throughout and only hold the position for 8-10 seconds, walking your feet back in and curling up through the body to come out of the stretch.

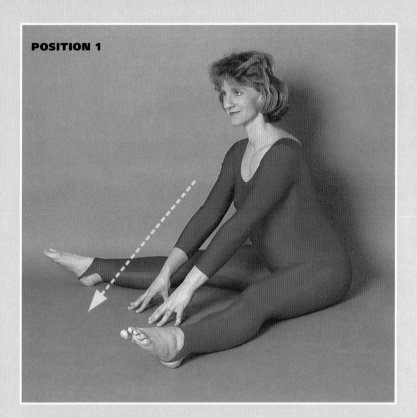

**POSITION 1**

**TOWEL TIP**

Using a towel can sometimes be a help; perhaps by wrapping it around your foot or leg when you cannot reach very far. Always try to keep your back straight and remember that you can still pull in on the stomach muscles, even if they are stretched beyond all recognition!

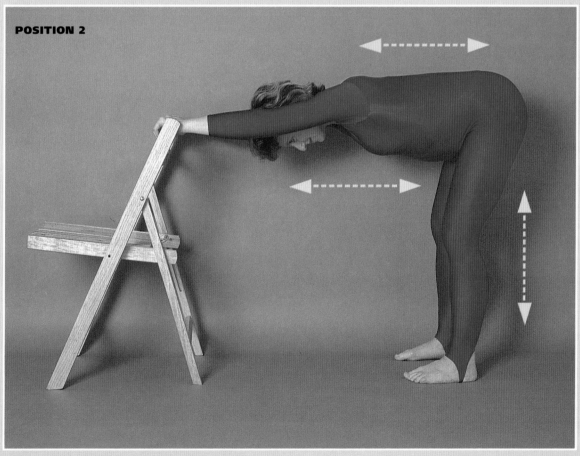

**POSITION 2**

# postnatal
# stretching

Congratulations! Now you have had your baby, you can start to remobilize areas of your body that haven't been used to moving. It is generally accepted that women can begin to work out properly after they have had their 6-week check up from the doctor.

As well as the stretches featured here you can also begin to include the warm-up section (Chapter 1) in your regime, as well as any of the beginners' stretches, to start challenging your whole body. Just remember to take it easy, and work slowly over the next three months to increase your general fitness – you should not feel any pain.

## AROUND THE MIDDLE

One of the prime areas that suffers from inactivity during pregnancy is the waist and middle torso. As the baby grew, your waist will have thickened and the chances are you have not done too much side bending and hip wiggling for the last few months. Now is the time to start! Side bends and revolving the hips can awaken the side of the torso and the oblique abdominal muscles, preparing them for the toning and strengthening exercises that you should also include in your postnatal work-out.

## POSITION 1:

Stand straight, with knees slightly bent and hips tucked under. Remember to pull in strongly on the stomach and lift the back now that you no longer have your bump! With hands on hips, slowly circle the hips anticlockwise, pushing them as far in each direction as you can. Then circle the other way.

• Repeat 6-7 times in each direction.

• Then wiggle the hips from side to side while bending the knees and repeat the circles once more.

POSITION 1

**POSITION 2**

## CRAMP AND PREGNANCY

Pregnant women can be particularly prone to cramp and this often occurs at night or on waking, and often in the feet and legs. Try doing the following gentle calf and ankle stretch before you go to sleep, or when you first wake:
• Stand with one hand resting against a wall and place one foot in front of the other. Now take all your weight onto the back foot (the other foot is still resting on the floor). Bend both knees gently until you feel a stretch at the back of the back leg. You can hold this stretch for up to 20 seconds and then straighten the legs to release. Repeat with the other leg in front. This position will help to stretch the lower calf muscle and the Achilles tendon area.
• Alternatively, standing on a low stair and letting the heels of both feet rest over the edge of the stair will also stretch out the calves. Keep the back straight and the abdominals pulled in.

## POSITION 2:

Something else you won't have done for a long time is lying on your tummy – so start trying it now. If you have had a caesarean, you may feel sore across the stomach, so approach this stretch very gently and if it feels too uncomfortable then leave it till a later date.

Once you are used to taking weight on your stomach again, try the following exercise: place your elbows underneath you and slowly lift your head and shoulders off the floor.
• This stretches the abdominals and mobilizes the lower back.

It is very important to look after your back post-natally – this is an area that is still much-affected by the Relaxin hormone and the strain of carrying and bearing a child makes it very unstable. A gentle mobilizing of the back, like this stretch, will help, along with some strengthening work.

## SAFETY NOTES

The relaxin hormone (see page 102) may still be present after you have given birth. It can stay in the body for at least 5 months if you are breastfeeding, so be aware that any stretching you do in the first 6 months must be done carefully and should not include the developmental stage.

# problem areas

## LEGS

When you are trying to stretch, or even simply carrying out everyday actions, you may find that one area is often stiffer than others and stiff legs is a common problem. Is lifting your leg to get over a fence difficult? Or is sitting up straight with both legs stretched out in front of you uncomfortable? This may be due to stiffness in the back of the legs (the hamstrings) or the groin area (the adductor muscles). If you do experience stiffness in these areas, it is worth spending extra time doing a variety of special stretches to increase your flexibility and rid yourself of any limiting restrictions in your daily movements.

## POSITION 1:

One of the best ways to develop your stretch is to adopt a position in which you can relax and so allow the muscles to start to lengthen. This position develops your groin stretch.

Lie on the floor with your backside as near the wall as you can manage and allow the legs to open equally to either side. Rest the legs fully against the wall and relax.

• The weight of your legs will start to stretch the muscles of the inner thighs as you maintain this position and you will feel a powerful but gradual stretch as you relax completely.

• Don't stay in this position for too long – 1-2 minutes is enough – and use your hands to push your legs together and roll out of the stretch.

• Gently knead or rub your inner thigh muscles to relieve them, then stand up and shake the legs out.

POSITION 1

## POSITION 2:

The splits position works on flexibility not just in the groin area but on the back of the legs and the front of the thighs too. You might think that the splits is beyond you, but if you approach the position gradually and attempt it regularly, you will notice the groin getting nearer and nearer to the floor. Try this with caution, and stop if you feel any pain.

The easiest and safest way to get into splits:
Start in the lunge position (page 38) and with hands on the floor, gently press the groin several times towards the floor. Now drop the knee of the back leg to the floor and place both hands on the front knee. Press the hips forward several times – so that you feel a stretch along the front of the thigh (of the back leg).

• Repeat 2 or 3 times , pressing slightly further each time.

Now tuck the back foot flat (so that the top of the foot is on the floor). With hands on the floor for support, slowly slide the back foot away from the front leg and let it take you down into the splits. Don't move the front leg at all but simply slide the back leg away from you as far as is comfortable.

• Hold for 10 seconds before releasing, shaking the legs out and trying the same on the other side.

• If you do this every day for 2 weeks you will be closer to the ground by at least a foot at the end of that time.

Other ways to stretch the back of the legs and groin area include:
• Placing one foot on a higher surface, for instance a chair or table, and leaning forwards over the straight leg. You will feel the stretch in the back of the raised leg.

• You can also place the leg in the same position but at the side of you, so that, as you lean over, you will feel the stretch in the side of the torso as well as the inner thigh.

• Once you have a leg raised on something stable, you can even lean over forwards, taking your hands onto the floor or letting them hang either side of the leg. In this way you will feel the stretch in the groin and the back of the supporting leg.

## BACK

Common back problems range from serious slipped discs and paralysis to constant aches and pains that remain unexplained but are nevertheless very tiresome. A lot of back problems, however, stem from misuse or lack of use of that area – especially bad posture.

The spine is actually designed to curve, bend and extend freely in all directions. It does not respond well to constant pressure from bad posture (slumping or leaning backwards on the lower back), stiffness from being forced and held in one position all the time (for instance if someone is always bent over a desk) or general inactivity.

Physiotherapists often remark that if people did more exercise, strength-ening and flexing the spinal area, then there would be far fewer back problems. If you develop a sore back or a nagging backache, try some gentle limbering exercises while you are waiting for an appointment with your doctor (take care, and stop if the stretches cause pain). These may well solve the problem and ease the tensions before you even make it to the surgery!

## POSITION 1:

One very relaxing back stretch is to lie on your back and bring the knees up towards your chest. Take your hands out to the side and rest them on the floor for balance. Now, keeping the knees together, tip the legs over to one side and rest them completely on the floor.

- Stay in this position for up to a minute and then swing the legs to the other side and rest there.
- This gently twists the spine and allows tension to seep away.

There are many variations on this stretch: you can swing one knee over with the other knee following, for example, which opens the hips out as you swing from side to side. You can also have one leg straight and take just one knee across the body towards the opposite side, which gives a slightly more intense twist in the spine. Experiment a little to see which position feels most comfortable and brings the most relief.

POSITION 1

**POSITION 2**

## POSITION 2:

This is a stretch specifically for the upper back.

Start by kneeling with both arms outstretched and resting on the floor. Rest your forehead on the floor and feel the release in your back as you maintain this pose for a while. Now thread one arm underneath and across the body and rest the side of your head on the floor.

• You will feel a relaxing stretch across the upper back.

• Hold for up to 1 minute and then repeat on the other side.

Other ways to stretch the back include lying on the back and bringing the feet into your chest, pressing the soles of the feet together, or even raise the legs up over the body so that only the shoulders remain on the floor. You will feel this stretch all along the back and the back of the legs. Move into and out of these positions slowly and only go as far as is comfortable.

## NECK AND SHOULDERS

The shoulders and neck area are often in need of regular stretching. Your smallish neck muscles not only support a heavy skull but also carry a lot of our general tension. It is always a good idea to get someone to massage this area gently on a regular basis and to learn how to stretch the head and neck area for yourself.

### POSITION 1:

Start by sitting with a straight back and place both your hands on the back of your head. Lift your elbows and press the head forwards as far as you can.

• Don't allow the back to curve or the stomach to sag; the torso should be fairly straight and lifted. Curve just from the base of the neck.
• As you hold this pose, you will feel the back of the neck stretching out.
• Hold for 10-15 seconds.

You can release the tension even further by keeping one hand on the top of your head and then using the first finger and thumb of the other hand to press lightly up the sides of the neck. Press the fingers in firmly all the way up to the base of the skull, right up into the hair, and down again. This will help release the tension that builds up in the back of the neck and across the shoulders.

### POSITION 2:

Now sitting straight, with abdominals lifted, tilt your head so that your left ear moves towards your left shoulder. Make sure that the shoulder is not lifted but is pressed down. Hold this for a few seconds and then take your left hand and gently place it on the side of your head to increase the stretch.

• Hold for 15 seconds then remove your hand and bring the head upright and repeat on the other side.
• This sequence will help to stretch and relieve the muscles at the side of the neck.

To continue this exercise, take the head forwards again and rest your chin on your chest. Use the fingers of

POSITION 1

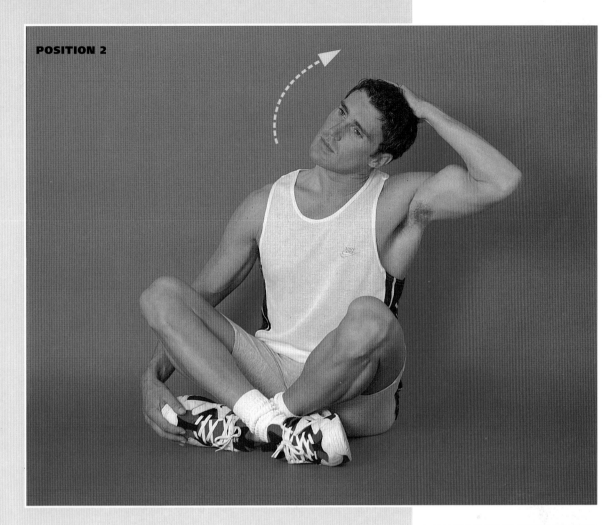

**POSITION 2**

both hands to press at intervals along the sides of the neck, right out to the top of the shoulders and back again. If you feel a particularly sore area, keep your fingers on it and massage in a circular motion to help release any knotted tension that might be lurking there.

• This will help release tension and stiffness along the trapezius muscle which runs across the shoulders and down the back (see pages 10-11).

## HEAD ROLLS

These are another good way to release the neck from tension and promote mobility in the neck and shoulder area. There is some controversy, however, over just how safe it

is to drop the head backwards. It is possible that this could lead to trapped nerves, but it should be remembered that the head does need to make this action from time to time, so it is better to practise it properly than to avoid it and risk the motion becoming stiff.

Make sure you circle your head with control (don't swing or fling it), slowly and smoothly. Start by taking the head forwards (chin to chest) and then roll it around to the side and gently to the back and around to the other side. Then repeat, taking the head in the other direction. Perform 4 or 5 head rolls until the "clicks" and "grinds" heard in the neck disappear.

# stretch for
# RELAXATION

CHAPTER 7

Stretching isn't just a way of increasing your fitness potential – it is also a highly pleasurable aid to relaxation. Stretching can release tension from shortened and over-stressed muscles and in this chapter you will find stretch positions that will let all kinds of tensions seep out of your mind and body.

If the body is held in rigid stances throughout the day, then placing it in the opposite position and allowing it to rest there can help the muscles "let go" and relax. After sitting down for a long time, for example, stretching can be just as relaxing as a hot bath. Perhaps you have had a long flight on an aeroplane or have been seated for hours at a conference – whatever the circumstances, stretching is one of the best ways to improve the circulation gently and loosen up the stiff areas, reawakening the body and preventing soreness from setting in.

In the previous chapter, you will have seen the stretches for problem areas – all of which help relieve tension in these vulnerable places. Even stretching in the bath or while watching T.V. will increase your sense of relaxation and well-being. Stretch

positions are usually better than simply lying flat out, because only slightly twisted positions can often give full relief to such areas as the upper back or buttocks.

### THE DOUBLE QUAD

Try, for example, adopting the position shown in the photograph. Lie on your front and reach behind you to take hold of both your ankles.

Grasp them firmly and then try to relax into the position. You will feel the stretch mainly on both upper thighs and across the hips. You will find that this is a particularly great way of relaxing the legs if you have been pounding the streets or going up and down stairs.

Let your hips sink towards the floor and turn your head to the side or rest your forehead on the floor if

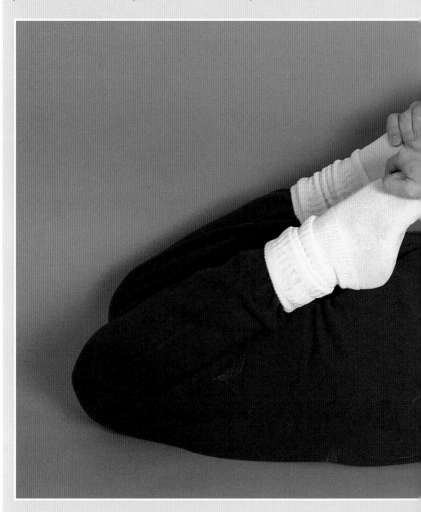

this is more comfortable. Keep your breathing regular and relaxed and enjoy the sensation of your leg muscles slowly extending and releasing their grip.

To come out of this stretch, simply release your hold on the ankles, and then use your hand to gently push yourself back onto all fours (knees and hands); massage the front of the thighs gently.

## GOING WITH THE FLOW

In this chapter you will also find some stretch routines that flow together. The purpose of these is to use your stretch as a way of moving smoothly and gently, in a way that will bring relaxation and pleasure. Once you have performed these routines several times, you will come to know them off by heart and you can do them as

little de-stress sessions during your day or just as a way of stretching out. You can also perform them with different goals in mind and with different music in the background, to really create a very specific mood-matching atmosphere. As you keep repeating these routines, you will be able to find different ways to make the most of them. So, Get stretching and get relaxing!

## STRETCH TO RELAX

Many relaxation techniques use tensing and stretching as a way to bring mind and body together and so aid total relaxation. Yoga uses many stretching postures that emphasize breathing and holding, so that the mind and body work in harmony. Dance, t'ai chi, and many other martial arts use stretching and relaxation side by side. When approaching your relaxation stretches, try to focus your mind on what your body is feeling. In this way you will achieve a clearness of mind and a relaxation of the body that will refresh you completely.

### STRETCH OUT

Try, for example, just lying flat on the floor on your back with your arms above your head. Now stretch out the whole body as far as you possibly can. Extend the legs from the hip joints and press right down through the knees to the toes. Feel your head and neck extending in the opposite direction and imagine the spaces between each vertebrae increasing as you stretch. You are growing!

Now release the stretch and just allow the body to sink back into the floor. Start to take note of which body areas are touching the floor and pressing down into it. Which limbs or part of limbs remain raised off the floor? Think through the body, starting at your head, and make sure that every part that could rest its weight on the floor is doing so.

Finally, take note again where your body touches the floor, working through bit by bit, and use the parts that touch as a focus for tension to disappear. Imagine that wherever the body touches the floor there is a

**EMBRYO STRETCH**

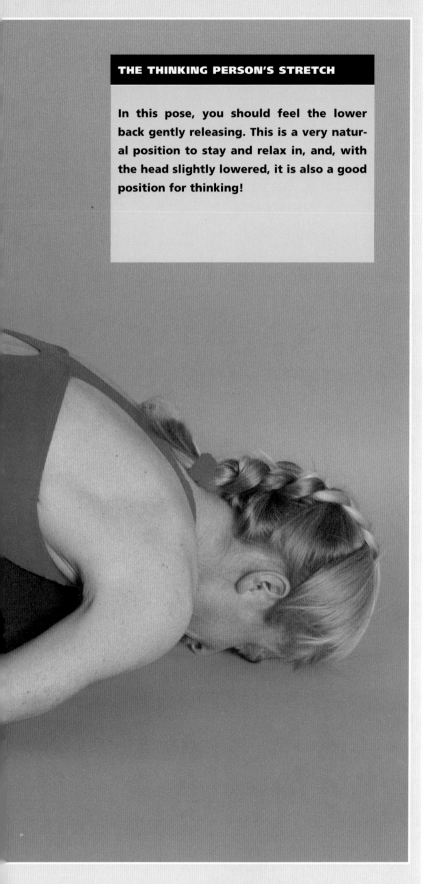

**THE THINKING PERSON'S STRETCH**

In this pose, you should feel the lower back gently releasing. This is a very natural position to stay and relax in, and, with the head slightly lowered, it is also a good position for thinking!

deep well below that draws out tension from the muscles and drains it into and beneath the floor. Repeat the stretch one more time and relax again afterwards.

## EMBRYO STRETCH

This is a great relaxation position to try when you are feeling tired out and, although it may not appear so, it will stretch and relieve your lower back. Start by kneeling low on the knees and stretch your arms out in front of you and rest the flat of the hands and the forehead on the floor. Your bottom should be nearly on your heels. Maintain this stretch for a while – here you will benefit from a stretch in the shoulders and arms as well as the lower and upper back.

Now gently bring the hands around to the sides of the body and rest here. This subtly changes the weight of the stretch, relaxing the lower back even further and putting slightly more weight on the forehead, which is also a good release point for tension.

## THE PRAWN STRETCH

To get into the pose shown in the photograph, take the following steps. Lie on your back with both arms out to the sides and legs straight down, relaxed on the floor. Lift your right leg up to the ceiling and then, keeping it as straight as possible, tilt the leg all the way over, so that your foot touches the opposite (left) hand. To accomplish this, the hips will have to tilt with you. Hold this stretch for 10-20 seconds to feel it across the back

and underneath the leg.

Now bend up the leg underneath (which at present is straight) and try and grasp its toes with your free hand. This may sound strange but once you are in position you can start to relax into it and will find that it is a very effective stretch.

Try to pull your two hands away from each other, gently, so that the two legs are being pulled in opposite directions. You should feel the stretch up the back of the top leg and across the groin and back, as

well as in the front thigh of the leg underneath. Try to stay in this position for 20-30 seconds, breathing easily and concentrating on letting the muscles relax into position and into the floor. Gently release your hold on both feet and slowly bring the legs back to their original position and rest briefly. Repeat on the other side.

After you have stretched both sides, hug your knees into your chest and rock gently from side to side to relax the hips and legs.

**THE PRAWN STRETCH**

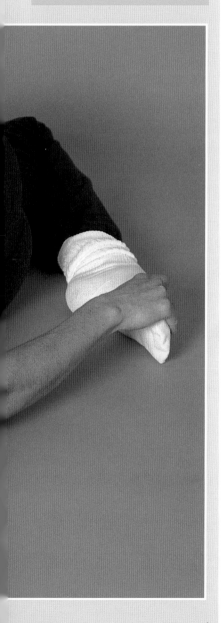

# stretching for life

Remember that you are never too young or too old to start stretching and keeping limber. As long as your programme of stretches is tailored to your needs and your body at that stage of life, and you exercise regularly, then there should be no injuries. All there should be is increased flexibility and pleasure in your movement.

## AN EARLY START

If you have children, encourage them to run around and make as much use of their limbs as possible. Gymnastic and dance classes are always a good idea to introduce your child some basic strength and flexibility work at an early age. The earlier children learn simple co-ordinating movements the better, and if they can learn to manipulate their own body weight, they will develop natural strength and agility that will help prevent accidents and stand them in good stead for the rest of their lives.

However, don't be over-zealous. A responsible teacher should not push your child beyond his or her natural limits at that age but should work with the natural mobility children have to bring co-ordination and fluidity to their movements.

Above all, early movement should be a source of pleasure and enjoyment for children who will then, hopefully, continue with the habit as they grow older.

## LATER LIFE

In the later years, stretching exercises are one of the best forms of preventive medicine. They keep joints mobile and help with balance and co-ordination as you get older. If you have been inactive for a long time, always check with your doctor before starting any kind of exercise programme and then start gradually and build up to longer, more energetic, sessions as you start to feel the benefits. As you are trying the stretches in this book, move into them all carefully and do not force anything. The stretch should feel challenging, but comfortable. The real test is whether the stretch is comfortable enough to maintain for up to 30 seconds if you had to. If you feel anything pulling or being twisted, then move to another stretch. Keep your stretches varied and make sure that they cover all areas of the body.

Try some swimming and walking to complement your stretching programme and only do what is comfortable. Switch to slightly different moves if certain stretches trouble you. But above all, remember that age is not a barrier and we can benefit at all ages from regular, easy movement.

# flexibility
# life-plan

## IN YOUR 20S

You're probably single and enjoying the freedom from studies and parents. You may have a big group of friends and, if you're working, some regular money for the first time. But this may also be the first time you are away from organized exercise (in school or college); you may also suddenly have a much more sedentary life if you're sitting in an office for long hours.

### HOW DO YOU FEEL ABOUT EXERCISE?

You may a feel a little de-motivated – there are so many other things to deal with – but your mustn't give up. Build it into your working life as quickly as you can. Exercise and keeping flexible should be fun in your 20s, a social event as well as a health necessity. Make sure your programme includes strength work, something that gets you running about a lot – and stretching!

### WHATS YOUR BODY DOING?

Heart and lung capacity (used in aerobic exercise) start to decline once you hit 25 – unless you work out regularly. Your bones reach their peak mass during your early 20s; you can maximise density with weight-bearing exercises (where you use your own body weight to strengthen your muscles, as in press-ups or squat thrusts) making bones stronger and helping to prevent osteoporosis later in life. You still burn calories at a good rate, so make the most of that to reach your target weight by the age of 30.

### STRETCH:

All areas of the body. Try to do at least 5-10 minutes, three times a week. Use all types of stretching methods (as described in this book) and have fun with it. Try attending stretching workshops or dance programmes that include flexibility work-outs.

## IN YOUR 30S

There is even more going on! You may be married, having children, forging busy careers. There never seems to be enough time. Beware – this is where the rot can really set in if you're not careful.

### HOW DO YOU FEEL ABOUT EXERCISE?

Guilty probably, unless you've kept it going since your 20s. You'd like to work out, but when you have the time you're too tired. You view exercise as a weapon to fight that getting-old feeling, but also as a chore.

### WHATS YOUR BODY DOING?

Your aerobic capacity is on the decline, so use it before you lose it. You are burning calories more slowly, so weight may be creeping on and affecting flexibility. You have already reached peak muscle mass, and will lose it unless you exercise. Your muscles are now less elastic and without regular stretching will become more prone to injury. If you have had children, your abdominal muscles may be slack and you may start to suffer from backache.

### STRETCH:

For 10 minutes each day (see programmes in Chapter 3) and include specific stretches for any particularly stiff areas (see Chapter 6). Include all types of stretches in your programme. Try some yoga or martial arts for a different kind of stretch.

## IN YOUR 40S

Job and family life have probably settled into some kind of routine. Children can amuse themselves a bit more and you may have a little more time to yourself. Your child-bearing years are waning and you may feel the need for a new focus in life.

### HOW DO YOU FEEL ABOUT EXERCISE?

Perhaps you'd feel out of place in an aerobics class (where the average age is 25). You may be carrying some extra weight and feel slower and more easily breathless. But don't despair – it's not too late to establish good habits and a regular regime. Starting now can improve your fitness later and will help blood flow, enhancing skin and muscle tone and even reversing some of the signs of ageing.

### WHATS YOUR BODY DOING?

Arms and breasts can start to sag without muscle toning exercises and lung capacity declines without regular aerobic work. Fat cells are stored on bottom, stomach and thighs, while a dramatic reduction in muscle protein means you can lose a lot of speed and strength if you don't work to keep it. You may feel stiffer if you haven't been doing your flexibility homework and might be experiencing the first signs of the menopause.

### STRETCH:

Everywhere you can, but keep it comfortable and avoid pushing or too many developmental stretches. Try to do 5-10 minutes as least twice a week. Concentrate on getting back any flexibility you feel you might have lost. Use this book to help you identify your stiff areas and then how to improve them and experiment with t'ai chi, gentle yoga class and relaxation techniques

## IN YOUR 50S & 60S

The children have left home so you have time for new interests. The menopause may have left you feeling a need to rethink your role in life.

### HOW DO YOU FEEL ABOUT EXERCISE?

You know it's important but you might have forgotten how or where to start!

### WHATS YOUR BODY DOING?

You're burning calories more slowly, so you need to eat less or opt for many more low-fat options in order to stay the same weight. You may feel weaker, particularly in the upper body and bone mass is lost rapidly, with a real risk of osteoporosis – weight bearing exercise where you use your own body weight to strengthen your muscles or work with dumbbells will help. Your joints will be stiffer and you will feel less flexible.

### STRETCH:

All parts of the body. Check everyday flexibility – can you reach up and down your back? Are you happy twisting right around to see behind you in the car? If the answer is no, then work on these areas first (See Chapters 1 & 2). Try to do at least 5-10 minutes three times a week and build up from there. Don't worry about too many developmental stretches; keep your routines comfortable and try some of the moving routines in this chapter for fun. Also try: stretches for relaxation (see this chapter) and brisk walking and swimming. Don't forget the benefits of massage as a way of rediscovering your muscles and the pleasure of relieving them.

# "wake up!"

This stretch routine is great for waking up in the morning – whatever age you are. It will get the blood flowing, the limbs moving and help you throw off that lingering sleepy feeling. If it appeals, you can do this to your favourite piece of music; make it rousing and upbeat if you have a busy morning ahead or just inspiring to set you up for the day.

## FEEL THE STRETCH

Hold each position long enough to feel the stretch in each muscle and then carry on moving onto the next movement. In this way you will start to memorize the routine so that you can perform it as a whole piece of choreography. Once you have become familiar with it (and the accompanying music), you can start to give different emphasis to different parts. For instance, you might want to prolong the reach-up at the beginning as you reach up high and fill your lungs with morning air. Or you might want to stay in position 3 to feel the legs really stretching out.

Whichever way you do it, put some energy and emotion into your stretches. Try to feel the music in your movement and fill the notes with long, sustained reaches of your limbs. Use your eyes to follow your hands or foot as it extends so that you are sending energy out beyond your body and across the room.

## POSITION 1:

• Reach both hands to the ceiling and stretch up through the spine as high as you can.

• Feel the pull through the spine and imagine the spaces between the vertebrae widening. Let the reach of your arms nearly pull you onto your toes.

• This stretches the spine all the way through to the neck.

• Let the hands start to arch you backwards so that you bend the spine gently. Keep the feeling of lift as you arch high.

• Only arch backwards as far as feels comfortable and keep the head supported rather then dropping it right back.

• This flexes the spine, particularly the lower back area and the neck.

## POSITION 2:

• From the arch position, stretch your arms to the sides as you bring them back down. Squeeze shoulder blades together to increase the stretch.

• Now sweep your right arm up and across your chest so that it leads the way as your shoulders twist rapidly to the left, turning your whole body to form a left-facing, sideways pose.

• Sink into a lunge, keeping your back leg as straight as possible, and take both hands and body over your front knee.

• Feel the stretch in the groin as you lower into the lunge. Keep the front knee directly in line with the toe and don't collapse the upper body over the leg. Hold in this position to increase the stretch.

• This stretches the shoulders, chest, groin and legs.

POSITION 2

**POSITION 3:**

**POSITION 4:**

## POSITION 3:

• From your lunge position, push the front knee to straighten the leg. Feel the back of the leg and straighten only as much as is bearable. Press the head towards the knee and then finally lift the front toes.

• You will feel a pull in the back of the legs as you perform this, so hold only as long as you are com-fortable and don't worry if you can't get your leg straight the first time.

• Flex the foot and bring the toes towards you to increase the stretch. This stretches the back of the legs and ankles.

## POSITION 5 AND 6:

• To complete this sequence, bend the front leg back into a lunge. Now twist the body towards your front leg, and keep on twisting in this direction, laying your back leg onto the floor. With your front leg bent, this will bring you into a sitting twist.

• Continue the twisting motion in the upper body to finish with the head and shoulders twisted even further round than the hips.

• Curl in tightly to make your curl as compact as possible and, with the final twist, feel the stretch in the waist. This stretches the torso and you will also feel it in the hips and legs.

Come up to a standing position and repeat the sequence on the other side – you should now be wide awake!

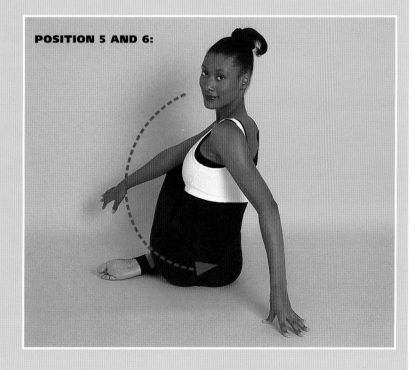

**POSITION 5 AND 6:**

# moving routines

These routines combine many basic stretches into flowing sequences that really give you a feeling for the way your body can move. Don't forget to use music to inspire you!

## BOOKENDS

This is a short moving routine that takes you through many of the basic stretching moves for legs and groin. Ease into each stretch gently and try to make all your movements as calm as possible. The transitions from one move to the next should be especially easy and smooth. Use music to help your movements flow and to reflect your mood.

Start in an upright position, facing the side of your room, and give yourself a quick posture check (see page 25). Now lift both arms to the ceiling, stretching up high and elongating the spine. Keeping your arms raised, slowly start to reach one leg back behind you into a low lunge. Keep the weight over your front leg as you stretch the other leg behind – this will help you keep your balance – and only settle the weight equally on both feet once you have your back leg well-placed behind you.
- Stretches groin and hamstrings

## POSITION 2:

From your lunge position, bring your arms down to rest your hands on the floor for support, either side of the bent leg. Then bring the arms in front of the bent leg and swivel to face the front of the room, keeping one leg bent and the other straight. This involves pressing the leg of the bent knee back as you turn in the hip. Your final position should be as in the photo, with both arms in front of the legs and both heels ideally touching the ground.
- This mobilizes the hip area and stretches the inner thigh muscles.

POSITION 1: BOOKENDS

POSITION 2

**POSITION 3**

**POSITION 4**

## POSITION 3:

Using your hands and the strength in your legs, simply push yourself over to the other side so that you end with the other leg bent, in a mirror image of position 2. Keep your backside and hips low to the ground as you swing across to the other side. This movement should feel smooth and unrestricted and you will feel more stretch in those inner thighs as

you move. Keeping the hands on the floor will support you, but as you get stronger and more flexible, try reaching your hands out in front of you so that all the work is done in the legs.

## POSITION 4:

From your side lunge, turn back into a forward facing lunge (you will now be facing the opposite direction to where you started), resting fingertips on the floor. Once again you are

swivelling in the hip and coming to rest in a low lunge.
• Stretches out the groin area.

## POSITION 5:

Keeping the left hip pressed forward, drop the knee of the back leg to the floor. Rest here a moment to feel an added stretch on the front of that thigh and then bend up the back leg. Reach your hand behind you to grasp the upturned foot and pull it towards your backside. Hold for 15 seconds.
• Puts a real stretch on the front of that back leg, which you should feel right up your torso.

Once you are at ease in this last position (and it is quite an advanced stretch), your sense of balance will improve. You could even try taking your front hand off the floor and posing! This is your bookend position, which calls for balance and flexibility at the same time.

• Don't forget to repeat the whole sequence going the other way, so that you end up stretching the other thigh.

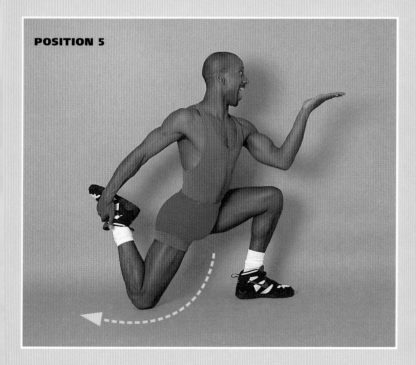

**POSITION 5**

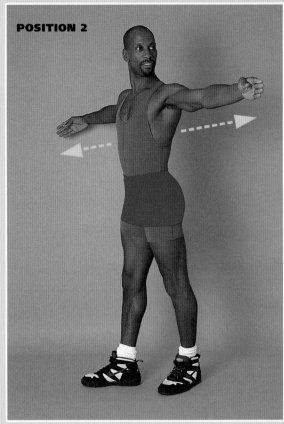

## "GET EMOTIONAL!"

This is your chance to put some real feeling into your movement. It is a simple stretch routine that you can learn easily and then interpret so that it is matched to your own ability and mood. Use the moves to express what you are feeling, whether it is frustration or joy. As you move your arms or legs, follow their path with your eyes and really extend your movements, sending the movement beyond your own body.

Put some stirring music on, find a place where you can be alone and get into it – express yourself! You'll be surprised at how liberating and relaxing the experience is.

## POSITION 1:

Start out standing tall, with the weight equally on both feet. After checking your posture (see page 7), slowly draw both arms up in front of you. As you raise the arms, try to imagine that the lift is coming right through the spine, making you so much taller that the top of your head presses against the ceiling.

Keep the arms "soft", that is, not straight and stiff but slightly rounded, with fingertips just touching. The torso should be well lifted via the abdominals but, again, not held rigid but relaxed, with the shoulder blades pressed down. Relax the facial muscles and think about sending the energy out well beyond your fingertips.

## POSITION 2:

Still keeping the arms soft, follow your hands with your eyes as the arms part and open to a wide position that you hold for a moment. Feel the muscles of the chest expanding as you press the arms open and put some strength into the motion as you open your arms and send the energy out through the ends of each finger.

Now take both arms up above your head, palms back to back, still following the hands with your eyes so that the back starts to arch slightly as you look upwards. Keep the torso lifted as you arch so that there is no pressure on the lower back.

**POSITION 3**

**POSITION 4**

## POSITION 3:

From this arched position, slide one leg back into a low lunge position and feel the stretch under the groin.
• This pose stretches the groin and the back of the legs.

## POSITION 4:

Once into the lunge, drop your back knee to the floor and, keeping the hips pressed forwards, twist the upper body to look behind you. Open up the arms from above your head and use them to help you twist, pulling the back hand onto the hip.

Turn your head to follow the line of your twist and gaze ahead.
• Mobilizes the waist and stretches the groin and the front of the back thigh.

## POSITION 5:

The grand finale – untwist the torso so that your bent arm comes back towards the front. Circle your right arm up in front, over your head and back behind you so that you can lean back and put your weight on it. To do this you must arch your back and push the hips forwards. With the other arm, make a half circle that reaches upwards to the sky in an emotive ending! The back is in as deep an arch as is comfortable, with one arm supporting you and the other stretching upwards.

Try this whole routine with the other leg, so that you feel the stretch on the other side. And don't forget that the more you do this, the easier it will become and the more emotion you can put into it!
• Mobilizes shoulders, back and hips.

**POSITION 5**

# stretch
# Index

Before going any further, the whole idea of stretch needs to be defined properly, especially as there are various common misconceptions about the subject. Stretching normally means elongating the muscles of the body. The muscles, tendons, ligaments and joint capsules of the body all stretch to varying degrees and this in turn can give an impression of the whole body feeling elongated, extended and lifted.

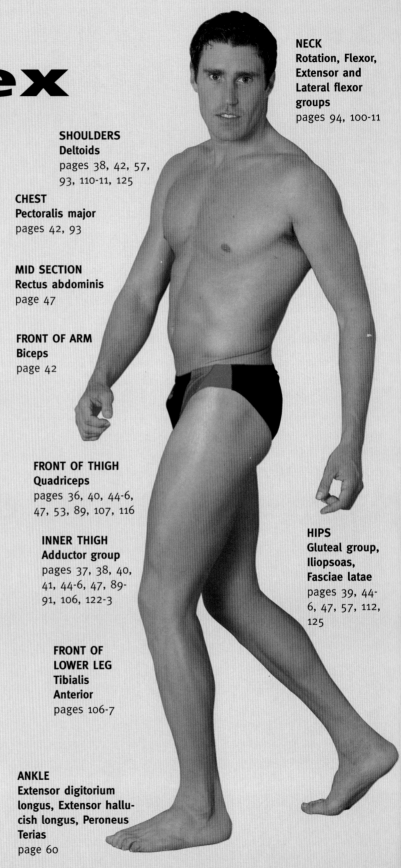

**NECK**
Rotation, Flexor, Extensor and Lateral flexor groups
pages 94, 100-11

**SHOULDERS**
Deltoids
pages 38, 42, 57, 93, 110-11, 125

**CHEST**
Pectoralis major
pages 42, 93

**MID SECTION**
Rectus abdominis
page 47

**FRONT OF ARM**
Biceps
page 42

**FRONT OF THIGH**
Quadriceps
pages 36, 40, 44-6, 47, 53, 89, 107, 116

**INNER THIGH**
Adductor group
pages 37, 38, 40, 41, 44-6, 47, 89-91, 106, 122-3

**HIPS**
Gluteal group, Iliopsoas, Fasciae latae
pages 39, 44-6, 47, 57, 112, 125

**FRONT OF LOWER LEG**
Tibialis Anterior
pages 106-7

**ANKLE**
Extensor digitorium longus, Extensor hallucish longus, Peroneus Terias
page 60

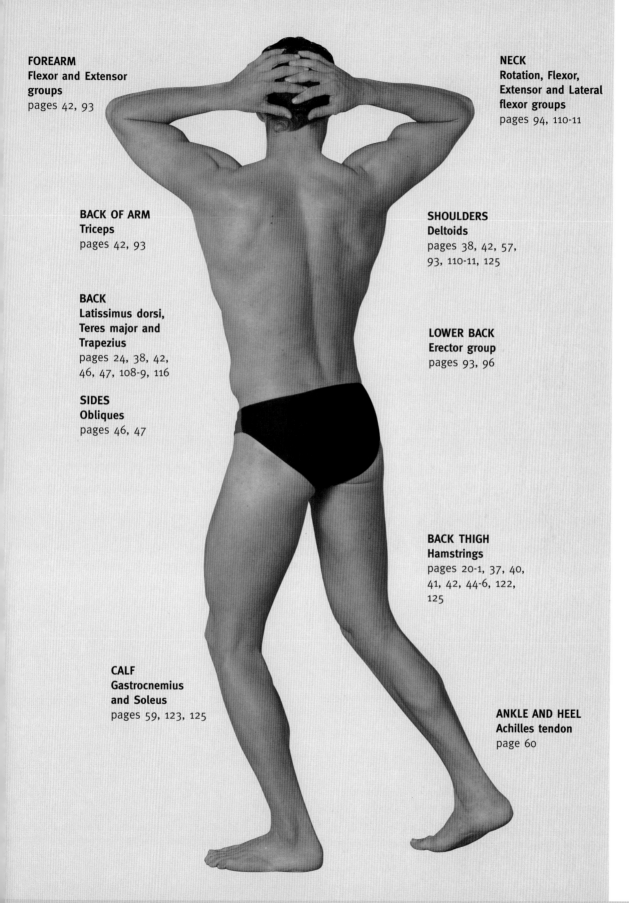

**FOREARM**
Flexor and Extensor
groups
pages 42, 93

**NECK**
Rotation, Flexor,
Extensor and Lateral
flexor groups
pages 94, 110-11

**BACK OF ARM**
Triceps
pages 42, 93

**SHOULDERS**
Deltoids
pages 38, 42, 57,
93, 110-11, 125

**BACK**
Latissimus dorsi,
Teres major and
Trapezius
pages 24, 38, 42,
46, 47, 108-9, 116

**LOWER BACK**
Erector group
pages 93, 96

**SIDES**
Obliques
pages 46, 47

**BACK THIGH**
Hamstrings
pages 20-1, 37, 40,
41, 42, 44-6, 122,
125

**CALF**
Gastrocnemius
and Soleus
pages 59, 123, 125

**ANKLE AND HEEL**
Achilles tendon
page 60

# Index